101 Easy Melodi(

MW00904323

Dear melodica player

I've collected 101 of my favourite popular and classic songs, and arranged them specifically for beginner melodica players.

All the songs are in easy keys, so you'll only have the occasional black note to play. I've put in some suggested finger numbers too, so you know which fingers to use for each note. There's also an image of a melodica for each song, showing you which notes you'll need to use.

If you're new to the melodica, have a read through the first few pages to see how it all works. And if you're rusty on your reading skills, check out the bonus theory section at the back of the book.

If you're struggling to read music, don't worry, I've written in the note names under every note. I've also added chord symbols above the music, for pianists, guitarists or other instruments.

Have fun, and if you get stuck, please ask for help on the MelodicaWorld Facebook group (facebook.com/groups/melodicaworld)

Daren Banarsë
Founder of MelodicaWorld.com

Also available on Amazon

Melodica Lessons Book One
melodicaworld.com/book

Scan here

Contents

About the melodica

Songs in order of difficulty

First published 2022 by Melodica World
Copyright © 2022 by Melodica World
All rights reserved.

Music theory

Join the Melodica World FaceBook community:
facebook.com/groups/melodicaworld

Scan
here

HOW TO USE THIS BOOK

All the songs in this book are arranged in order of difficulty, starting from the easiest and ending with the more challenging.

The first 9 pages are an introduction to the melodica, taken from the tutor book, 'Melodica Lessons, Book One"

The first 10 songs (pages 11-21) are the easiest, because they use a fixed hand position - each finger is assigned to its own note.

In the rest of the songs, the hand position changes throughout the piece. Have a look at the musical scale on page 23 to see how the thumb is used to seamlessly connect hand positions together.

To make sure you don't run out of fingers while playing, work out which fingers will play which note before you start practising. I've added little finger numbers above some of the notes - feel free to add some more with a pencil.

The letters in the boxes above the score are called chord symbols. They're for guitarists, pianists or teachers, so they know which chords to use while accompanying you. You can ignore these!

WHAT SIZE IS YOUR MELODICA?

WHAT SIZE IS YOUR MELODICA?

Melodicas come in many different shapes and sizes. The most common are 32 key and 37 key.

32 key

37 key

5 Extra notes

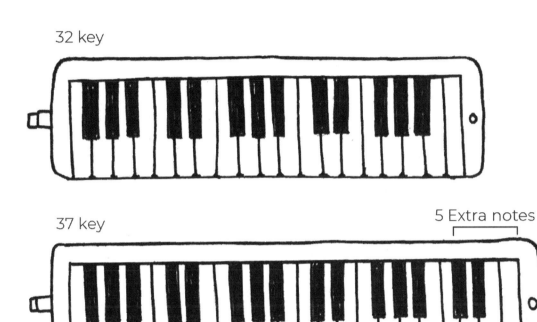

YOUR HAND

Each finger has its own number, starting with the thumb, which is finger number 1.

2 3 4 5 1

It's easier to play with short fingernails

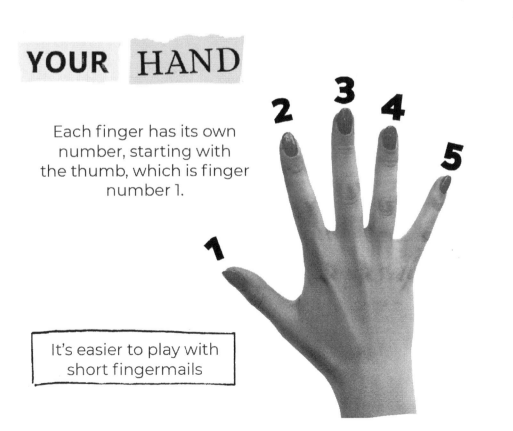

PLAYING POSITION

Place the melodica on a table in front of you, with your feet flat on the floor. Make sure the chair is square to the table. Lean slightly forward in a relaxed upright position. In this position, with the hose connected, you can see where all the keys are.

When you get more advanced, you can use the mouthpiece. Hold the melodica with your left hand, and play with the right. This is great for walking while playing, but you can only use one hand, and won't be able to see the keyboard!

HAND POSITION

With the melodica in front of you, let your hand drop gently onto the keyboard. If it's relaxed, it should land in a curved shape.

There's no fixed position when playing, the most important thing is to stay relaxed. If you notice tension building, take a break and slow it down, until you're playing in a way that's comfortable.

INSIDE THE MELODICA

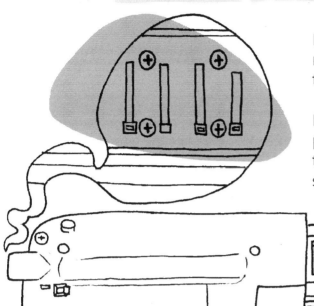

If you remove enough screws, you'll reach the reed chamber, deep inside the melodica.

Here you'll find some long metal plates with a series of delicate metal tongues attached. There's a different size tongue for every note.

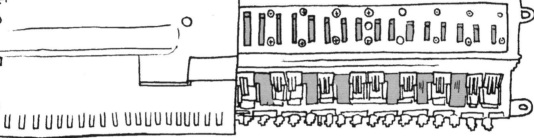

The larger the reed, the lower the note, and the more air it takes to sound.

HOW IT WORKS

When you blow into the melodica and press a key, air is directed towards one of many tuned metal tongues. The tongue vibrates and shapes the air into a pattern, which creates the sound.

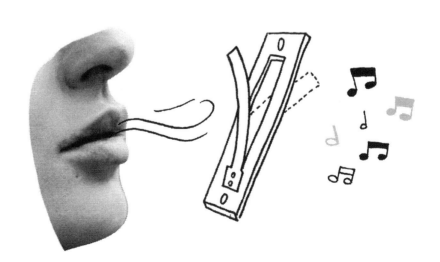

The breatH

Connect one end of the hose to the melodica, and hold the other end between your lips. When you need to take a breath, take air in through the nose. Press a key while blowing to make a sound.

If you blow gently, you'll produce a soft sound, and if you blow with more force, you'll make a strong sound. Always decide what quality of sound you want to produce, before blowing. **Listen carefully to the sound, to check it's how you intended it to be.**

Keep any key pressed down, and use your breath to begin making the following sounds:

1) A long soft sound
2) A short loud sound

Play around with different breathing styles, and see how many variations in tone you can make. **Notice how the quality of the breath effects the sound of the melodica.** This is what makes it such an expressive instrument.

BREATH CONDENSATION

After a few minutes of playing, condensation from the hot breath starts to collect on the cold metal reeds inside, making the pitch very slightly lower.

When too much moisture collects up, notes can make strange sounds, go out of tune, or stop playing altogether. To avoid this happening you can release the moisture by pressing the button at the end and blowing it out.

NAMES OF THE KEYS

Melodica keys are named with the first seven letters of the alphabet, beginning with A.

To find an A, look for any group of 3 black notes. Play the white key between the 2nd and 3rd black keys.

Here's all the A notes on a 32 key melodica

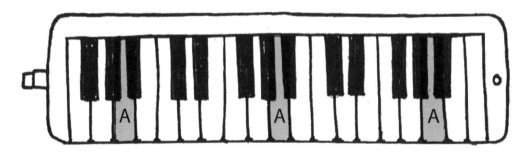

Once you know where the A notes are, you can work out the other key names, following the alphabet.

101 Songs

The first 10 songs are the easiest to play, because the hand stays in one position.

Use the image of the melodica at the bottom of the page to see where to place the hand. Each finger rests over its own note.

If you need help with reading the music, turn to the music theory section at the back of the book.

HOT CROSS BUNS

Traditional

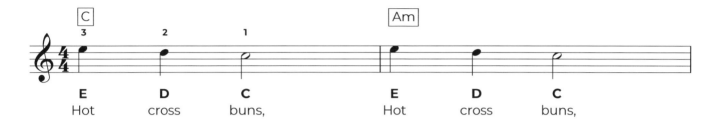

Hot   cross   buns,   Hot   cross   buns,

One   a   pen - ny,   two   a   pen - ny,   Hot   cross   buns

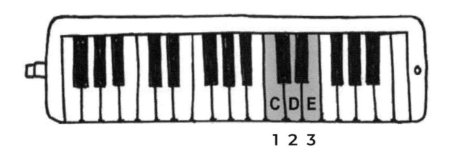

12

MARY HAD A LITTLE LAMB

Traditional

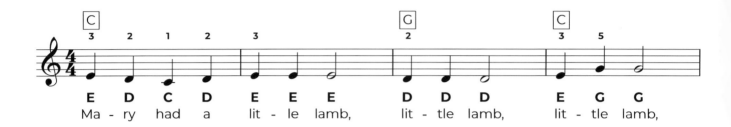

E D C D E E E | D D D | E G G
Ma - ry had a lit - tle lamb, lit - tle lamb, lit - tle lamb,

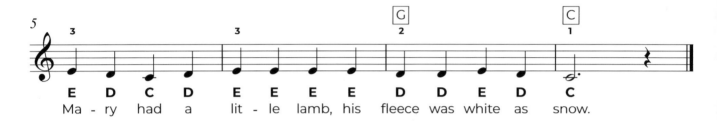

E D C D E E E E | D D E D | C
Ma - ry had a lit - tle lamb, his fleece was white as snow.

2 Everywhere that Mary went,
Mary went, Mary went,
Everywhere that Mary went,
The lamb was sure to go.

3 It followed her to school one day,
School one day, school one day,
It followed her to school one day,
Which was against the rules.

4 It made the children laugh and play,
Laugh and play, laugh and play,
It made the children laugh and play,
To see a lamb at school.

5 And so the teacher turned it out,
Turned it out, turned it out,
And so the teacher turned it out,
But still it lingered near.

6 And waited patiently about,
Patiently about, patiently about,
And waited patiently about,
Till Mary did appear.

7 "Why does the lamb love Mary so?
Love Mary so? Love Mary so?
Why does the lamb love Mary so?"
The eager children cry.

8 "Why, Mary loves the lamb, you know.
Loves the lamb, you know, loves the lamb, you know,
Why, Mary loves the lamb, you know."
The teacher did reply.

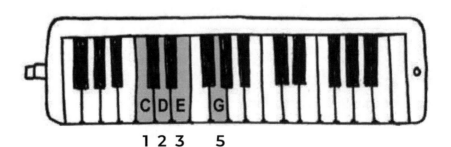

When the Saints go Marching In

Traditional

2 Oh, when the drums begin to bang,
Oh, when the drums begin to bang,
Oh Lord I want to be in that number,
When the saints go marching in.

3 Oh, when the stars fall from the sky,
Oh, when the stars fall from the sky,
Oh Lord I want to be in that number,
When the saints go marching in.

4 Oh, when the moon turns red with blood,
Oh, when the moon turns red with blood,
Oh Lord I want to be in that number,
When the saints go marching in.

5 Oh, when the trumpet sounds its call,
Oh, when the trumpet sounds its call,
Oh Lord I want to be in that number,
When the saints go marching in.

6 Oh, when the horsemen begin to ride,
Oh, when the horsemen begin to ride,
Oh Lord I want to be in that number,
When the saints go marching in.

7 Oh, brother Charles you are my friend,
Oh, brother Charles you are my friend,
Yea, you gonna be in that number,
When the saints go marching in.

8 Oh, when the saints go marching in,
Oh, when the saints go marching in,
Oh Lord I want to be in that number,
When the saints go marching in.

Catalina Magdalena

Russian folk song

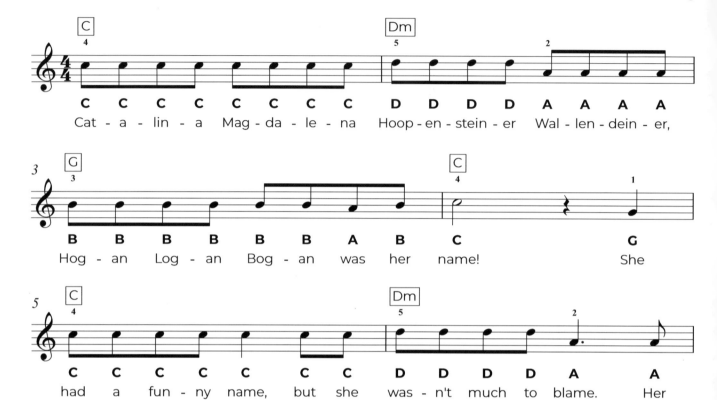

C								Dm				A			
C	C	C	C	C	C	C	C	D	D	D	D	A	A	A	A
Cat	- a	- lin	- a	Mag	- da	- le	- na	Hoop	- en	- stein	- er	Wal	- len	- dein	- er,

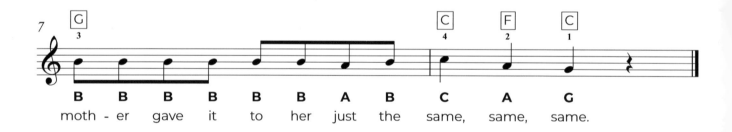

G								C		
B	B	B	B	B	B	A	B	C		G
Hog	- an	Log	- an	Bog	- an	was	her	name!		She

C							Dm					
C	C	C	C	C	C	C	D	D	D	D	A	A
had	a	fun	- ny	name,	but	she	was	- n't	much	to	blame.	Her

G								C	F	C
B	B	B	B	B	B	A	B	C	A	G
moth	- er	gave	it	to	her	just	the	same,	same,	same.

G A B C D

1 2 3 4 5

2 Catalina Magdalena Hoopensteiner Wallendiner
Hogan Logan Bogan was her name.
Well, she had two peculiar hairs on her head,
One was black and one was red.

3 Catalina Magdalena Hoopensteiner Wallendiner
Hogan Logan Bogan was her name.
She had two eyes that were quite a sight,
One looked left and the other looked right.

4 Catalina Magdalena Hoopensteiner Wallendiner
Hogan Logan Bogan was her name.
She had two arms that flopped all around,
When she walked, they would drag on the ground.

5 Catalina Magdalena Hoopensteiner Wallendiner
Hogan Logan Bogan was her name.
She had two feet that were wide and flat,
Each one bigger than a bathroom mat.

6 Catalina Magdalena Hoopensteiner Wallendiner
Hogan Logan Bogan was her name.
She had two holes in the bottom of her nose,
One for her fingers ....and one for her toes.

7 Catalina Magdalena Hoopensteiner Wallendiner
Hogan Logan Bogan was her name.
She had two teeth inside her mouth,
One went north and the other south.

8 Catalina Magdalena Hoopensteiner Wallendiner
Hogan Logan Bogan was her name.
Some folks say her breath smells sweet,
But me, I'd rather smell her feet.

9 Catalina Magdalena Hoopensteiner Wallendiner
Hogan Logan Bogan was her name.
If rain makes flowers sweet and clean,
There oughta be a downpour on Magdaleen!

LITTLE BIRCH TREE

Russian folk song

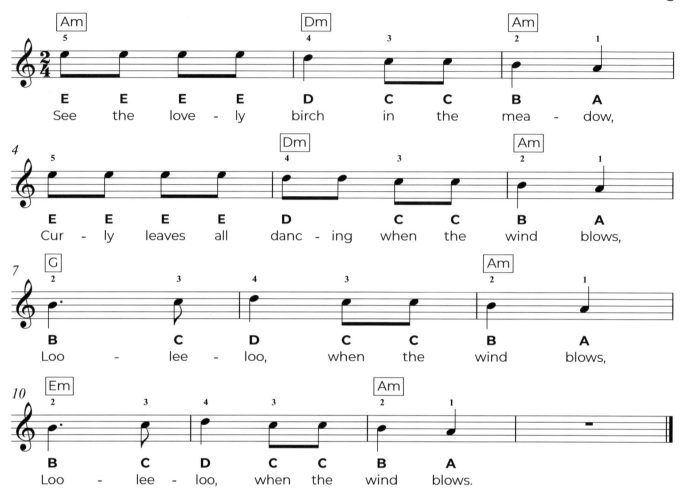

See the love - ly birch in the mea - dow,

Cur - ly leaves all danc - ing when the wind blows,

Loo - lee - loo, when the wind blows,

Loo - lee - loo, when the wind blows.

2 Oh, my little tree, I need branches,
For the silver flutes I need branches.
Loo-lee-loo, three branches,
Loo-lee-loo, three branches.

3 From another birch I will make now,
I will make a tingling balalaika.
Loo-lee-loo, balalaika,
Loo-lee-loo, balalaika.

4 When I play my new balalaika,
I will think of you, my lovely birch tree.
Loo-lee-loo, lovely birch tree,
Loo-lee-loo, lovely birch tree.

Yoo Hoo

Folk song

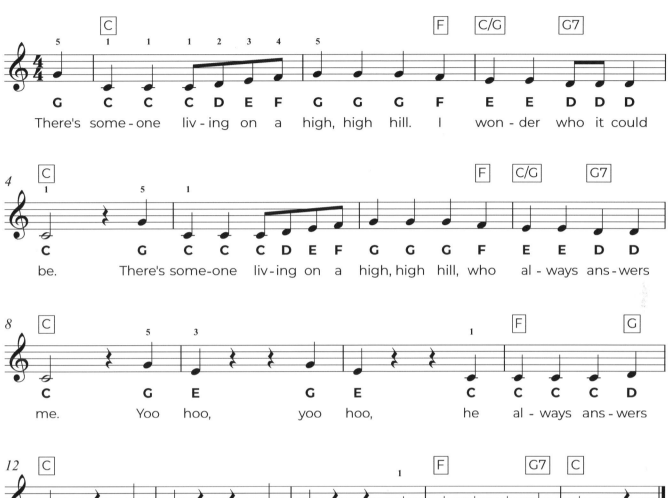

There's some-one liv-ing on a high, high hill. I won-der who it could be. There's some-one liv-ing on a high, high hill, who al-ways ans-wers me. Yoo hoo, yoo hoo, he al-ways ans-wers

me. Yoo hoo, yoo hoo, he al-ways ans-wers me.

C D E F G

1 2 3 4 5

MERRILY WE ROLL ALONG

Traditional

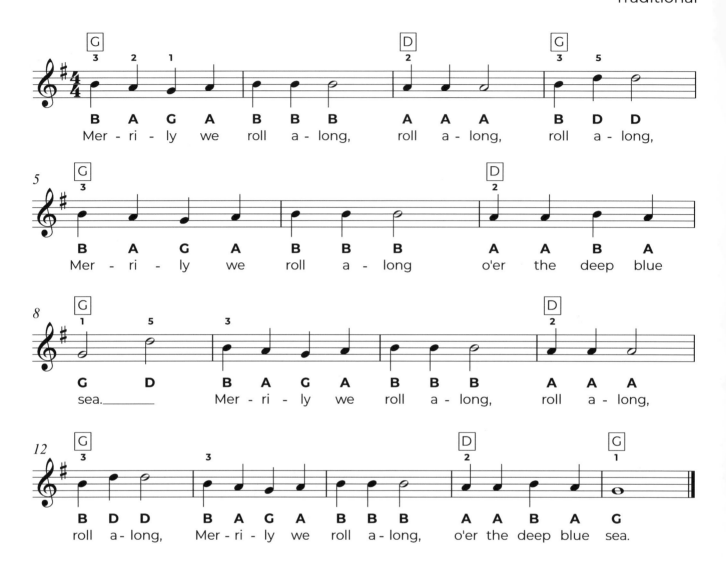

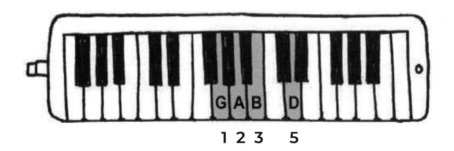

HUSH LITTLE BABY

Traditional

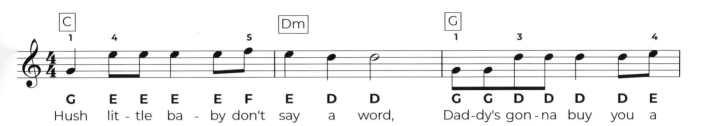

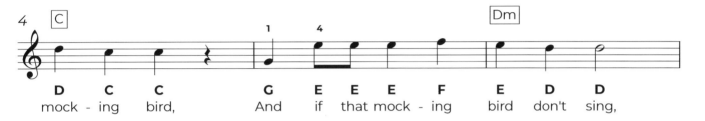

2 And if that diamond ring turns brass,
Papa's gonna buy you a looking glass,
And if that looking glass gets broke,
Papa's gonna buy you a billy goat.

3 And if that billy goat won't pull,
Papa's gonna buy you a cart and bull,
And if that cart and bull turn over,
Papa's gonna buy you a dog named Rover.

4 And if that dog named Rover won't bark,
Papa's gonna buy you a horse and cart,
And if that horse and cart fall down,
You'll still be the sweetest little baby in town.

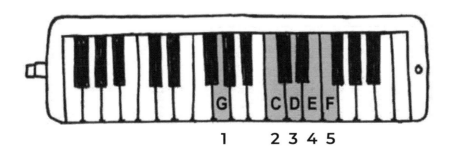

OLD DAN TUCKER

Traditional

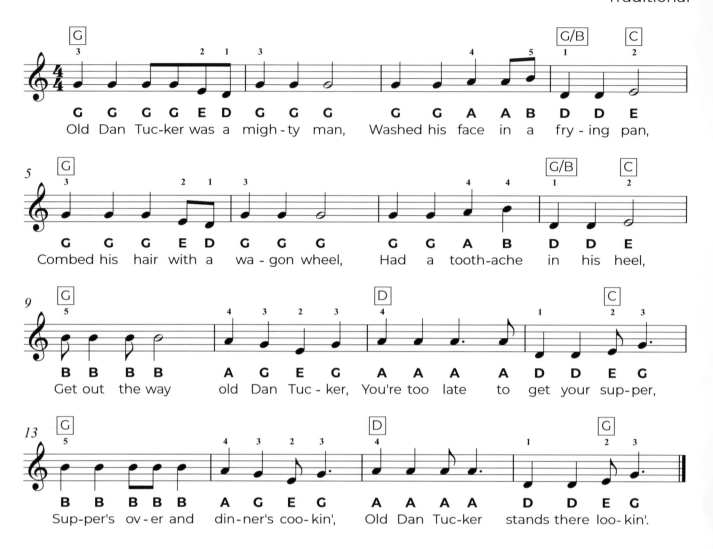

Old Dan Tuc-ker was a migh-ty man, Washed his face in a fry-ing pan,

Combed his hair with a wa-gon wheel, Had a tooth-ache in his heel,

Get out the way old Dan Tuc-ker, You're too late to get your sup-per,

Sup-per's ov-er and din-ner's coo-kin', Old Dan Tuc-ker stands there loo-kin'.

2 Old Dan Tucker came to town,
Riding a billy-goat, leading a hound,
Hound dog barked and the billy-goat jumped,
Dan fell off and landed on a stump.
Get out the way old Dan Tucker,
You're too late to get your supper,
Supper's over and dinners cookin',
Old Dan Tucker stands there lookin.'

3 Old Dan Tucker came to town,
To hear a noise and see the fight,
Watchman's feet was a-running 'round,
Crying "Old Dan Tucker's come to Town."
Get out the way old Dan Tucker,
You're too late to get your supper,
Supper's over and dinners cookin',
Old Dan Tucker stands there lookin.'

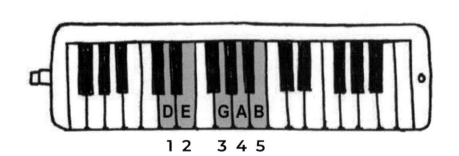

Old MacDonald Had a Farm

Traditional

2 Old MacDonald had a farm,
Ee i ee i o,
And on that farm he had some chicks,
Ee i ee i o.
With a cluck-cluck here,
And a cluck-cluck there,
Here a cluck, there a cluck,
Everywhere a cluck-cluck,
Old MacDonald had a farm,
Ee i ee i o.

3 Old MacDonald had a farm,
Ee i ee i o,
And on that farm he had some pigs,
Ee i ee i o.
With an oink-oink here,
And an oink-oink there,
Here an oink, there an oink,
Everywhere an oink-oink,
Old MacDonald had a farm,
Ee i ee i o

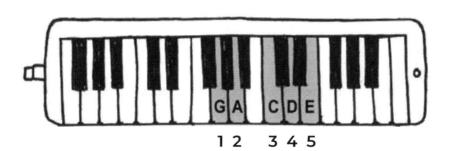

FLUID HAND POSITION

The rest of the songs require a fluid hand position, where the hand moves around the keyboard to play the required notes.

You can do this by working out which finger will play which note before practising the song. This will ensure you don't run out of fingers, and help with smooth transitions between positions.

I've put some numbers above some of the notes, indicating which fingers to use. Feel free to add your own with a pencil.

Try playing the musical scale on the following page, to see how the thumb is used to connect two different positions together smoothly.

C Major Scale

The C major scale begins on a C and goes up to another C, before coming down again. There are no sharps or flats in the C major scale, they are all white notes.

Playing all the notes in this scale requires the hand to move from a lower position to a higher position, and then back to a lower position.

Begin with the thumb on C, with each finger resting on the adjacent notes. **(1)**

After you play the 3rd note, slide the thumb under the fingers to play the F. **(2)**

With the F note pressed, move the rest of the fingers into the new position. The thumb should now be on F, with each finger resting on the adjacent notes. **(3)**

On the way back down, once you reach the F, lift the 3rd finger over the thumb **(2)** and return to the 1st position. **(1)**

Moving your fingers like this might feel stiff at first, but with practice you'll develop flexibility in the thumb, and it will become much easier.

(1) (2) (3)

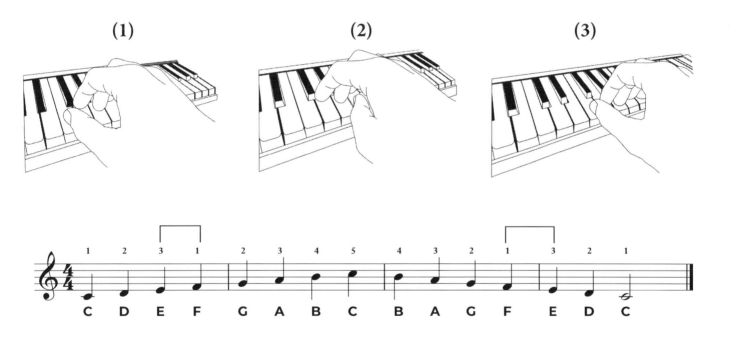

1 2 3 1 2 3 4 5

Are You Sleeping (Frere Jacques)

Traditional

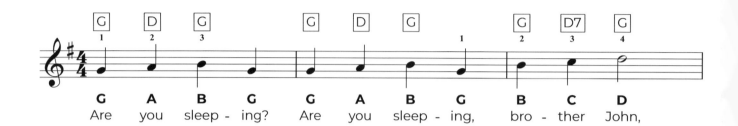

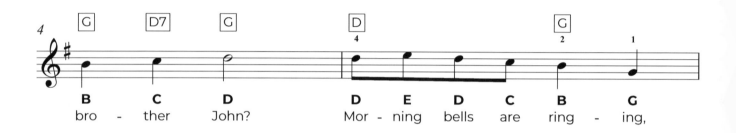

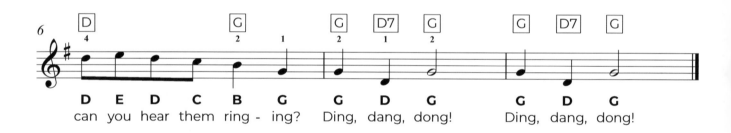

THIS OLD MAN

Traditional

C 4 2 4 — — **F** 5 4 3 2

G E G G E G A G F E
This old man, he played one. He play knick - knack

G 1 — — — — **C** 4 1

D E F E F G C C C C
on my thumb, With a knick - knack pad - dy wack,

6 1 5 **G** 2 4 **G7** **C** 1

C D E F G G D D F E D C
Give the dog a bone, This old man came roll - ing home.

2 This old man, he played two,
He played knick-knack on my shoe;
With a knick-knack…

3 This old man, he played three,
He played knick-knack on my knee;
With a knick-knack…

4 This old man, he played four,
He played knick-knack on my door;
With a knick-knack…

5 This old man, he played five,
He played knick-knack on my hive;
With a knick-knack…

6 This old man, he played six,
He played knick-knack on my sticks;
With a knick-knack…

7 This old man, he played seven,
He played knick-knack up in heaven;
With a knick-knack…

8 This old man, he played eight,
He played knick-knack on my gate;
With a knick-knack…

9 This old man, he played nine,
He played knick-knack on my spine;
With a knick-knack…

10 This old man, he played ten,
He played knick-knack once again;
With a knick-knack…

JACK AND JILL

Traditional

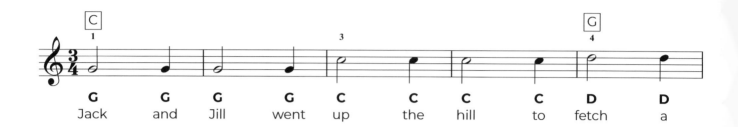

Jack and Jill went up the hill to fetch a

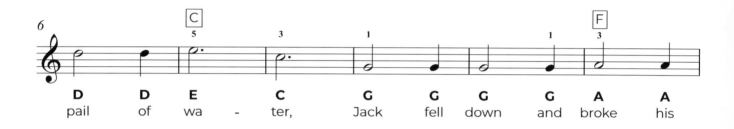

pail of wa - ter, Jack fell down and broke his

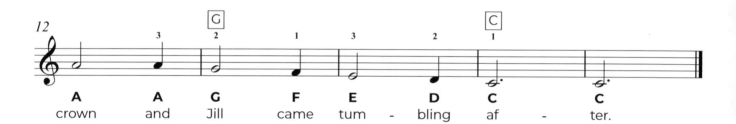

crown and Jill came tum - bling af - ter.

2 Then up got Jack and said to Jill,
As in his arms he took her,
"Brush off that dirt for you're not hurt,
Let's fetch that pail of water."

3 So Jack and Jill went up the hill
To fetch the pail of water,
And took it home to Mother dear,
Who thanked her son and daughter.

The Itsy Bitsy Spider

Traditional

Humpty Dumpty

Traditional

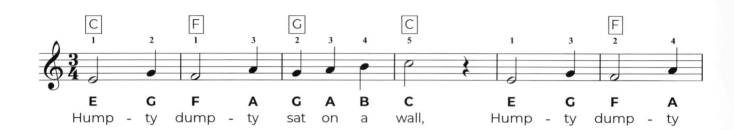

Hump - ty dump - ty sat on a wall, Hump - ty dump - ty

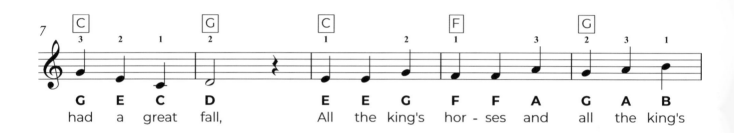

had a great fall, All the king's hor - ses and all the king's

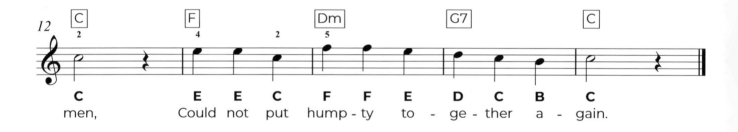

men, Could not put hump - ty to - ge - ther a - gain.

HAPPY BIRTHDAY TO YOU

Traditional

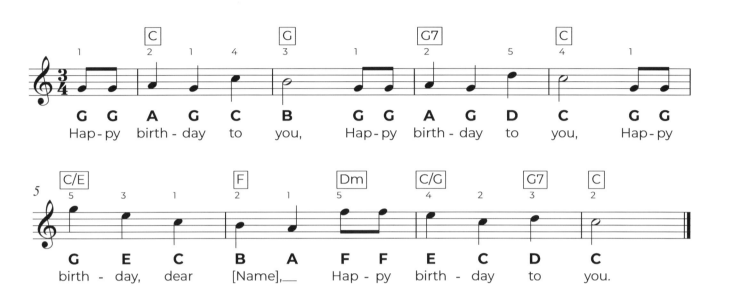

2 From good friends and true,
From old friends and new,
May good luck go with you,
And happiness too.

SILENT NIGHT

Franz Xaver Gruber

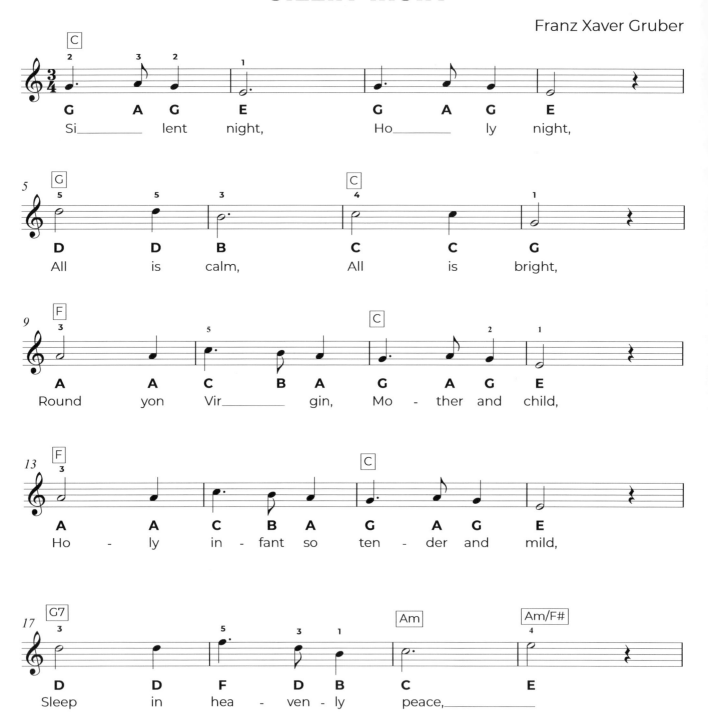

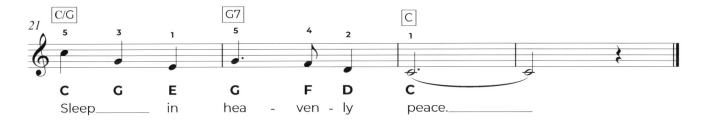

Sleep_____ in hea - ven - ly peace._____

2 Silent night, holy night!
Shepherds quake at the sight.
Glories stream from heaven afar
Heavenly hosts sing Alleluia,
Christ the Saviour is born!
Christ the Saviour is born

3 Silent night, holy night!
Son of God love's pure light.
Radiant beams from Thy holy face
With dawn of redeeming grace,
Jesus Lord, at Thy birth
Jesus Lord, at Thy birth

4 Silent night! Holy night!
Where on this day all power
of fatherly love poured forth
And like a brother lovingly embraced
Jesus the peoples of the world,
Jesus the peoples of the world.

5 Already long ago planned for us,
When the Lord frees from wrath
Since the beginning of ancient times
A salvation promised for the whole world.
A salvation promised for the whole world.

6 Silent night! Holy night!
To shepherds it was first made known
By the angel, Alleluia;
Sounding forth loudly far and near:
Jesus the Saviour is here!
Jesus the Saviour is here!

NIPA HOMES

Traditional

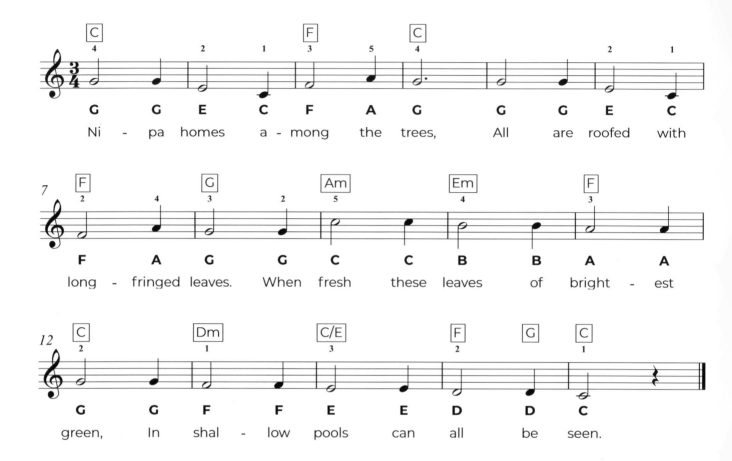

Ni - pa homes a - mong the trees, All are roofed with long - fringed leaves. When fresh these leaves of bright - est green, In shal - low pools can all be seen.

2 Folded leaves will soon be dry,
Underneath a tropic sky,
When bound upon a bamboo frame,
shelter folks from sun and rain.

THREE BLIND MICE

Traditional English

Twinkle Twinkle Little Star

Traditional

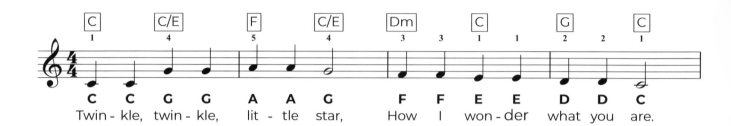

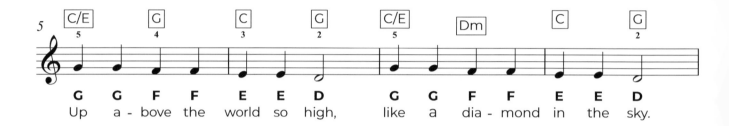

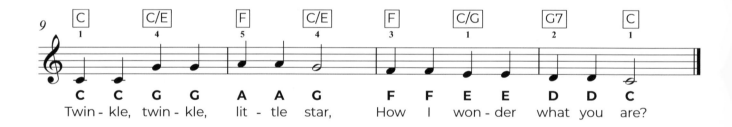

DONKEYS AND CARROTS

Belgian folk song

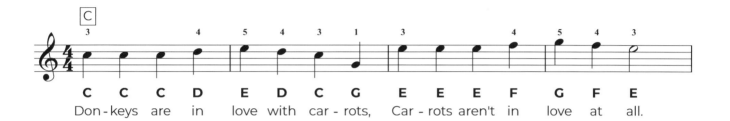

C C C D E D C G E E E F G F E
Don - keys are in love with car - rots, Car - rots aren't in love at all.

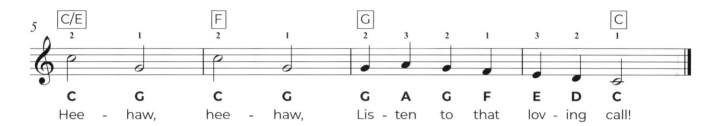

C G C G G A G F E D C
Hee - haw, hee - haw, Lis - ten to that lov - ing call!

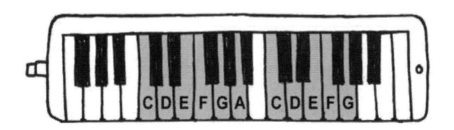

London Bridge is Falling Down

Traditional

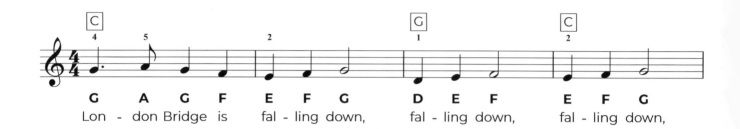

G A G F E F G D E F E F G
Lon - don Bridge is fal - ling down, fal - ling down, fal - ling down,

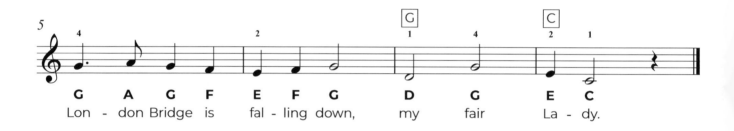

G A G F E F G D G E C
Lon - don Bridge is fal - ling down, my fair La - dy.

I LIKE TO EAT

Traditional

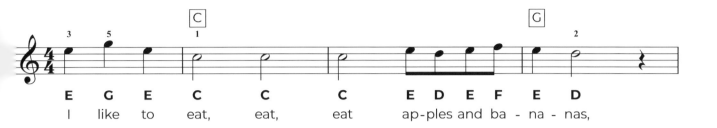

E G E C C C E D E F E D
I like to eat, eat, eat ap-ples and ba - na - nas,

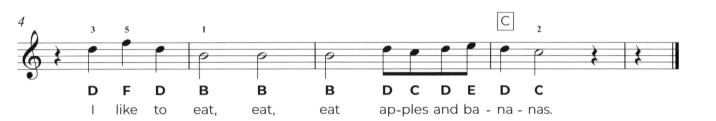

D F D B B B D C D E D C
I like to eat, eat, eat ap-ples and ba - na - nas.

A
A lake to ate, ate, ate ay-ples and ba-nay-nays,
A lake to ate, ate, ate ay-ples and ba-nay-nays.

E
E leke to eat, eat, eat ee-ples and bee-nee-nees,
E leke to eat, eat, eat ee-ples and bee-nee-nees.

I
I like to ite, ite, ite i-ples and by-ny-nys,
I like to ite, ite, ite i-ples and by-ny-nys.

O
O loke to ote, ote, ote oh-ples and bo-no-nos,
O loke to ote, ote, ote oh-ples and bo-no-nos.

U
U luke to oot, oot, oot oo-ples and boo-noo-noos,
U luke to oot, oot, oot oo-ples and boo-noo-noos.

Blow the Man Down

Traditional shanty

2 She was round in the counter and bluff in the bow,
Way hey blow the man down,
So I took in all sail and cried, "Way enough now,"
Oh gimme some time to blow the man down.

3 I hailed her in English, she answered me clear,
Way hey blow the man down,
"I'm from the Black Arrow bound to the Shakespeare,"
Oh gimme some time to blow the man down.

4 So I tailed her my flipper and took her in tow,
Way hey blow the man down,
And yardarm to yardarm away we did go,
Oh gimme some time to blow the man down.

5 But as we were going she said unto me,
Way hey blow the man down,
There's a spanking full-rigger just ready for sea,
Oh gimme some time to blow the man down.

6 That spanking full-rigger to New York was bound,
Way hey blow the man down,
She was very well manned and very well found,
Oh gimme some time to blow the man down.

7 And as soon as that packet was out on the sea,
Way hey blow the man down,
`Twas devilish hard treatment of every degree,
Oh gimme some time to blow the man down.

8 But as soon as that packet was clear of the bar,
Way hey blow the man down,
The mate knocked me down with the end of a spar,
Oh gimme some time to blow the man down.

9 It's starboard and larboard on deck you will sprawl,
Way hey blow the man down,
For Kicking Jack Williams commands the Black Ball,
Oh gimme some time to blow the man down.

10 So I give you fair warning before we belay,
Way hey blow the man down,
Don't ever take heed of what pretty girls say,
Oh gimme some time to blow the man down.

11 A bonnie good mate and a captain too,
Way hey blow the man down,
A bonnie good ship and a bonnie good crew,
Oh gimme some time to blow the man down.

12 Blow the man down, bullies, blow the man down,
Way hey blow the man down,
Blow the man down, bullies, pull him around,
Oh gimme some time to blow the man down.

13 Blow the man down, you darlings, lie down,
Way hey blow the man down,
Blow the man down for fair London town,
Oh gimme some time to blow the man down.

14 When the Black Baller is ready for sea,
Way hey blow the man down,
That is the time that you see such a spree,
Oh gimme some time to blow the man down.

15 There's tinkers, and tailors, and soldiers and all,
Way hey blow the man down,
They all ship for sailors on board the Black Ball,
Oh gimme some time to blow the man down.

16 When the Black Baller hauls out of the dock,
Way hey blow the man down,
To see these poor fellows, how on board they flock,
Oh gimme some time to blow the man down.

17 When the Black Baller gets clear of the land,
Way hey blow the man down,
'Tis then you will hear the great word of command,
Oh gimme some time to blow the man down.

18 'Lay aft here, ye lubbers, lay aft, one and all,
Way hey blow the man down,
I'll none of your dodges on board the Black Ball,
Oh gimme some time to blow the man down.

19 To see these poor devils, how they will all 'scoat,'
Way hey blow the man down,
Assisted along by the toe of a boot,
Oh gimme some time to blow the man down.

20 It's now we are sailing on th' ocean so wide,
Way hey blow the man down,
Where the deep and blue waters dash by our black side,
Oh gimme some time to blow the man down.

21 It's now when we enter the channel so wide,
Way hey blow the man down,
All hands are ordered to scrub the ship's side,
Oh gimme some time to blow the man down.

22 And now, my fine boys, we are round the rock,
Way hey blow the man down,
And soon, oh! soon, we will be in the dock,
Oh gimme some time to blow the man down.

23 Then all our hands will bundle ashore,
Way hey blow the man down,
Perhaps some will never to sea go more,
Oh gimme some time to blow the man down.

KUM BA YAH

Traditional

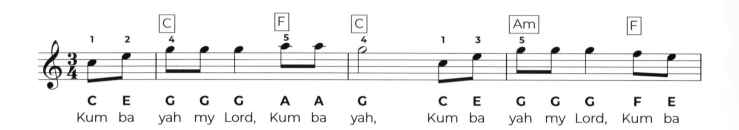

C E G G G A A G — Kum ba yah my Lord, Kum ba yah,

C E G G G F E — Kum ba yah my Lord, Kum ba

D — yah, C E G G G A A G — Kum ba yah my Lord, Kum ba yah,

F E C D D C — Oh Lord_ Kum ba yah

2 Someone's crying, Lord, Kum ba yah,
Someone's crying, Lord, Kum ba yah,
Someone's crying, Lord, Kum ba yah,
O Lord, Kum ba yah.

3 Someone's singing, Lord, Kum ba yah,
Someone's singing, Lord, Kum ba yah,
Someone's singing, Lord, Kum ba yah,
O Lord, Kum ba yah.

4 Someone's praying, Lord, Kum ba yah,
Someone's praying, Lord, Kum ba yah,
Someone's praying, Lord, Kum ba yah,
O Lord, Kum ba yah.

APPLE TREE

French folk song

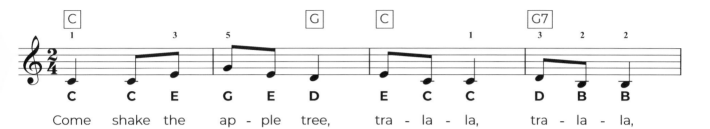

Come shake the ap - ple tree, tra - la - la, tra - la - la,

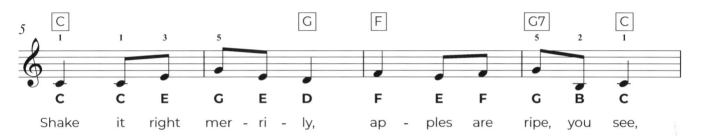

Shake it right mer - ri - ly, ap - ples are ripe, you see,

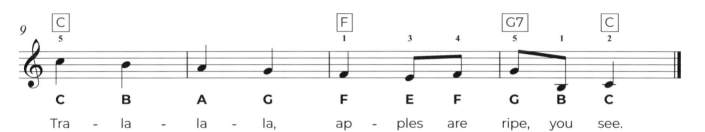

Tra - la - la - la, ap - ples are ripe, you see.

2 Apples enough for all,
Tra la la, tra la la,
Growing in branches tall,
Pattering and pelting fall,
Tra la la la,
Pattering and pelting fall.

3 Gather a goodly store,
Tra la la, tra la la,
Full baskets, three or four,
Still there'll be many more,
Tra la la la,
Still there'll be many more.

4 Pleased will dear mother be,
Tra la la, tra la la,
All our ripe fruit to see,
Apples we'll have for tea,
Tra la la la,
Apples we'll have for tea.

Row, Row, Row Your Boat

Traditional

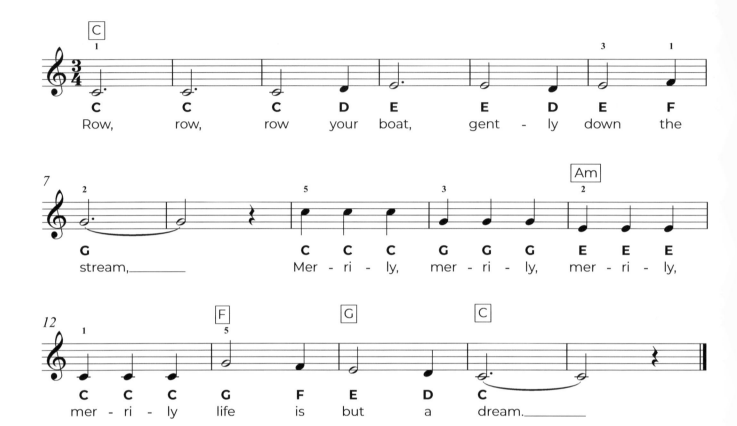

C

Row, row, row your boat, gent - ly down the

C C C D E E D E F

G

stream,_____ Mer - ri - ly, mer - ri - ly, mer - ri - ly,

C C C G G G E E E Am

mer - ri - ly life is but a dream._____

C C C G F E D C F G C

B-I-N-G-O

Traditional

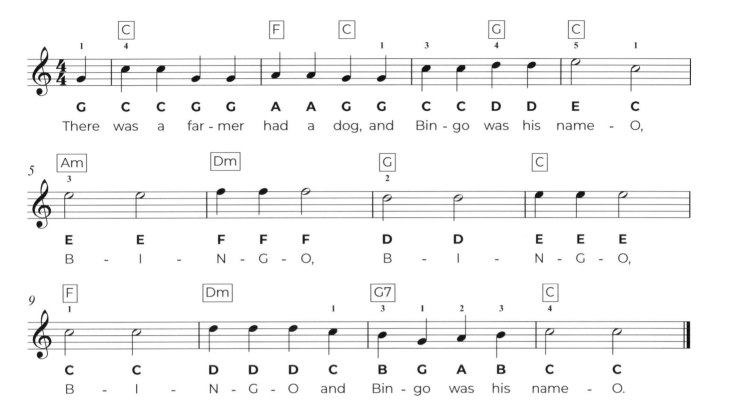

2 There was a farmer who had a dog,
and Bingo was his name-O.
(clap)-I-N-G-O
(clap)-I-N-G-O
(clap)-I-N-G-O
And Bingo was his name-O.

3 There was a farmer who had a dog,
and Bingo was his name-O.
(clap)-(clap)-N-G-O
(clap)-(clap)-N-G-O
(clap)-(clap)-N-G-O
And Bingo was his name-O.

4 There was a farmer who had a dog,
and Bingo was his name-O.
(clap)-(clap)-(clap)-G-O

(clap)-(clap)-(clap)-G-O
(clap)-(clap)-(clap)-G-O
And Bingo was his name-O.

5 There was a farmer who had a dog,
and Bingo was his name-O.
(clap)-(clap)-(clap)-(clap)-O
(clap)-(clap)-(clap)-(clap)-O
(clap)-(clap)-(clap)-(clap)-O
And Bingo was his name-O.

6 There was a farmer who had a dog,
and Bingo was his name-O.
(clap)-(clap)-(clap)-(clap)-(clap)
(clap)-(clap)-(clap)-(clap)-(clap)
(clap)-(clap)-(clap)-(clap)-(clap)
And Bingo was his name-O.

CROCODILE SONG

Canadian folk song

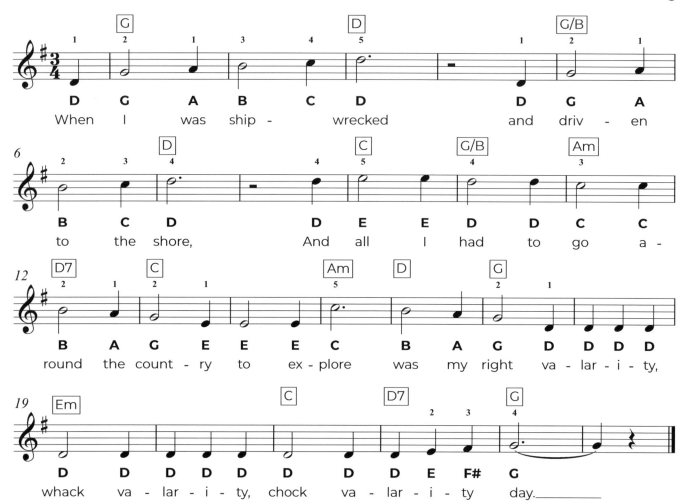

When I was ship - wrecked and driv - en to the shore, And all I had to go a - round the count - ry to ex - plore was my right va - lar - i - ty, whack va - lar - i - ty, chock va - lar - i - ty day._____

2 And steering up the other side,
I found the crocodile,
From the tip of his nose to the end of his tail,
He was ten thousand miles with a...
Right valarity, whack valarity, chock valarity day.

3 The crocodile, you see,
Was not of common race,
I had to climb up a very tall pine,
To look into his face with a...
Right valarity, whack valarity, chock valarity day.

4 I bore away from his head one day,
With every stitch of the sail,
And going nine knots by the log,
In ten months reached his tail with a...
Right valarity, whack valarity, chock valarity day.

5 The crocodile set his mouth,
And thought he had his victim,
But I went down his throat, you see
And that is how I tricked 'im with a...
Right valarity, whack valarity, chock valarity day.

AURA LEE

Composer: George R Poulton
Lyrics: W W Fosdick

2 In thy blush the rose was born,
Music, when you spake,
Through thine azure eye the morn,
Sparkling seemed to break.
Aura Lea, Aura Lea,
Birds of crimson wing,
Never song have sung to me,
As in that sweet spring.

3 Aura Lea! the bird may flee,
The willow's golden hair
Swing through winter fitfully,
On the stormy air.

Yet if thy blue eyes I see,
Gloom will soon depart;
For to me, sweet Aura Lea
Is sunshine through the heart.

4 When the mistletoe was green,
Midst the winter's snows,
Sunshine in thy face was seen,
Kissing lips of rose.
Aura Lea, Aura Lea,
Take my golden ring;
Love and light return with thee,
And swallows with the spring.

BLUEBIRD, BLUEBIRD

American folk song

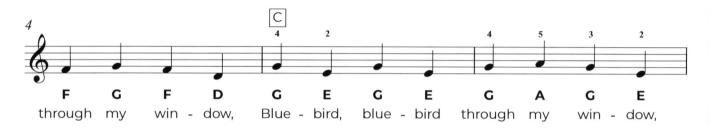

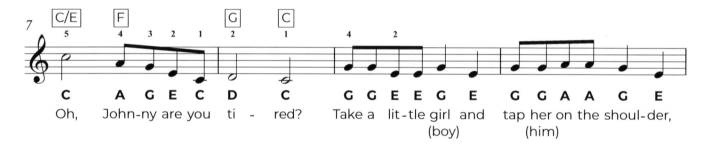

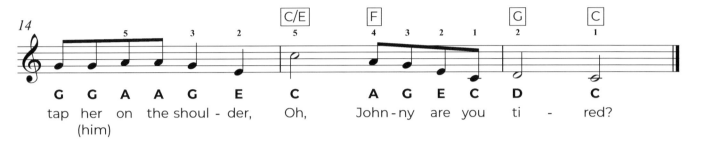

tap her on the shoul - der, Oh, John - ny are you ti - red?
(him)

2 Bluebird, bluebird through my window,
Bluebird, bluebird through my window,
Bluebird, bluebird come through my window,
Oh, Johnny, I am tired.

Take a little boy and tap him on the shoulders,
Take a little boy and tap him on the shoulders,
Take a little boy and tap him on the shoulders,
Oh, Johnny, I am tired!

For He's a Jolly Good Fellow

Traditional

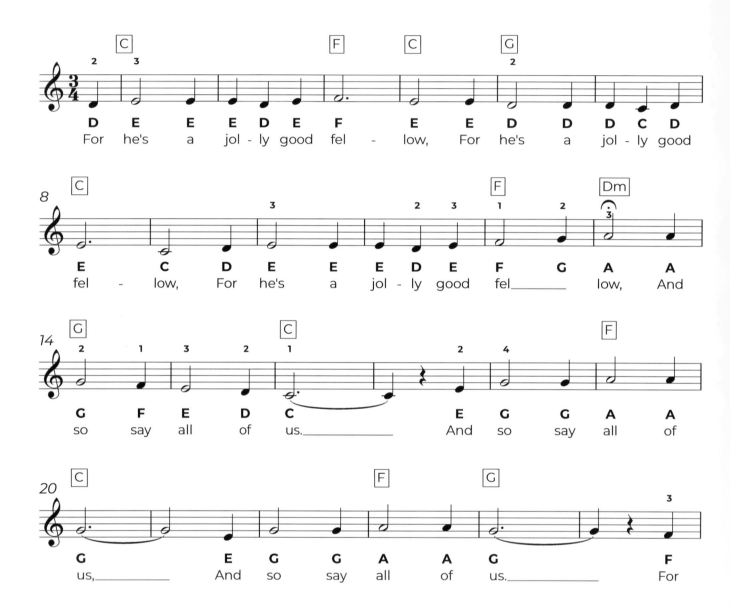

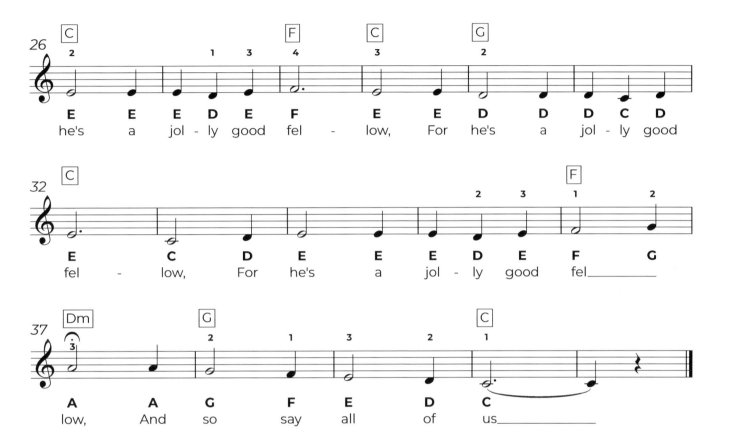

Yankee Doodle

Traditional

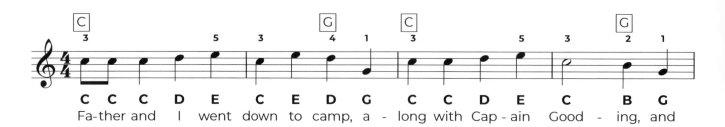

C C C D E | C E D G | C C D E | C | B G
Fa-ther and I went down to camp, a - long with Cap - ain Good - ing, and

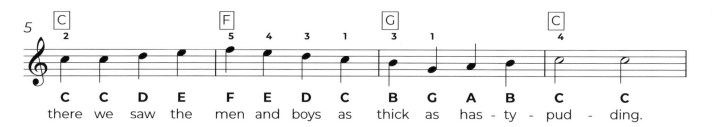

C C D E | F E D C | B G A B | C C
there we saw the men and boys as thick as has - ty - pud - ding.

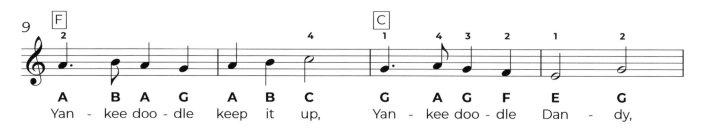

A B A G | A B C | G A G F | E G
Yan - kee doo - dle keep it up, Yan - kee doo - dle Dan - dy,

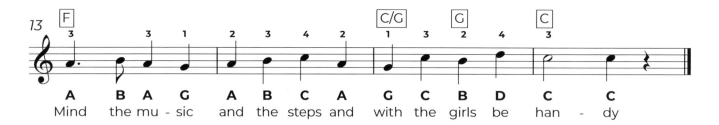

A B A G | A B C A | G C B D | C C
Mind the mu - sic and the steps and with the girls be han - dy

2 There was Captain Washington
Upon a slapping stallion,
A-giving orders to his men,
I guess there was a million.
Yankee doodle...

3 And then the feathers on his hat,
They looked so' tarnal fin-a,
I wanted pockily to get,
To give to my Jemima.
Yankee doodle...

4 And then we saw a swamping gun,
Large as a log of maple,
Upon a deuced little cart,
A load for father's cattle.
Yankee doodle...

5 And every time they shoot it off,
It takes a horn of powder,
It makes a noise like father's gun,
Only a nation louder.
Yankee doodle...

6 I went as nigh to one myself,
As' Siah's underpinning,
And father went as nigh agin,
I thought the deuce was in him.
Yankee doodle...

7 We saw a little barrel, too,
The heads were made of leather,
They knocked upon it with little clubs,
And called the folks together.
Yankee doodle...

8 And there they'd fife away like fun,
And play on cornstalk fiddles,
And some had ribbons red as blood,
All bound around their middles.
Yankee doodle...

9 The troopers, too, would gallop up,
And fire right in our faces,
It scared me almost to death,
To see them run such races.
Yankee doodle...

10 Uncle Sam came there to change,
Some pancakes and some onions,
For' lasses cake to carry home,
To give his wife and young ones.
Yankee doodle...

11 But I can't tell half I see,
They kept up such a smother,
So I took my hat off, made a bow,
And scampered home to mother.
Yankee doodle...

12 Cousin Simon grew so bold,
I thought he would have cocked it,
It scared me so I streaked it off,
And hung by father's pocket.
Yankee doodle...

13 And there I saw a pumpkin shell,
As big as mother's basin,
And every time they touched it off,
They scampered like the nation.
Yankee doodle...

BOBBY SHAFTO

Traditional

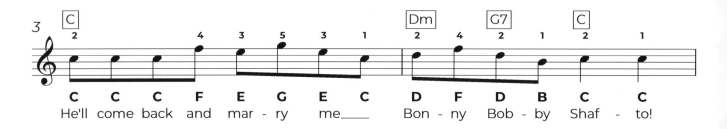

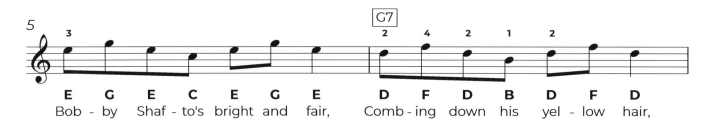

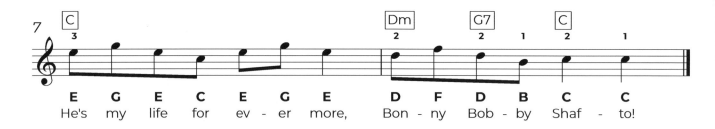

Oh My Darling Clementine

Lyrics: Percy Montross

In a cav - ern, in a can - yon, ex - ca - vat - ing for a mine, Dwelt a

min - er for - ty nin - er, and his daugh - ter Clem-en - tine. Oh my

dar - ling, oh my dar - ling, oh my dar - ling Clem-en - tine! Thou art

lost and gone for - ev - er dread-ful sor - ry, Clem-en - tine.

2 Light she was and like a fairy,
And her shoes were number nine,
Herring boxes, without topses,
Sandals were for Clementine.

Oh my darling, oh my darling...

3 Drove she ducklings to the water,
Ev'ry morning just at nine,
Hit her foot against a splinter,
Fell into the foaming brine.

Oh my darling, oh my darling...

4 Ruby lips above the water,
Blowing bubbles, soft and fine,
But, alas, I was no swimmer,
So I lost my Clementine.

Oh my darling, oh my darling...

5 How I missed her! How I missed her,
How I missed my Clementine,
But I kissed her little sister,
I forgot my Clementine.

Oh my darling, oh my darling...

BIM BUM

American folk song

If You're Happy and You Know it

Traditional

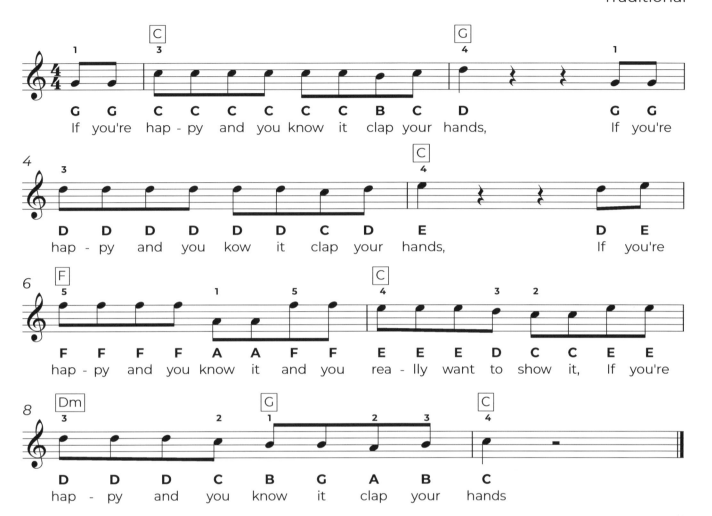

G G | C C C C C C B C | D | G G
If you're hap-py and you know it clap your hands, If you're

D D D D D D C D | E | D E
hap-py and you kow it clap your hands, If you're

F F F F A A F F | E E E D C C E E
hap-py and you know it and you rea-lly want to show it, If you're

D D D C B G A B | C
hap-py and you know it clap your hands

2 If you're happy and you know it,
Stamp your feet.
If you're happy and you know it,
Stamp your feet.
If you're happy and you know it,
And you really want to show it,
If you're happy and you know it,
Stamp your feet.

3 If you're happy and you know it,
Nod your head.
If you're happy and you know it,
Nod your head.

If you're happy and you know it,
And really want to show it,
If you're happy and you know it,
Nod your head.

4 If you're happy and you know it,
Jump about.
If you're happy and you know it,
Jump about.
If you're happy and you know it,
And you really want to show it,
If you're happy and you know it,
Jump about.

Oh Susanna

Stephen Foster

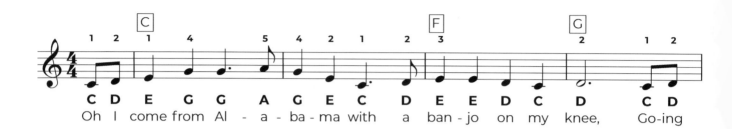

Oh I come from Al - a - ba - ma with a ban - jo on my knee, Go-ing

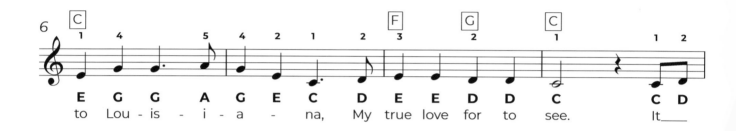

to Lou - is - i - a - na, My true love for to see. It___

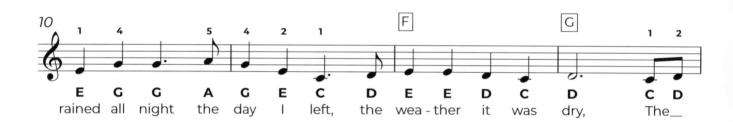

rained all night the day I left, the wea - ther it was dry, The__

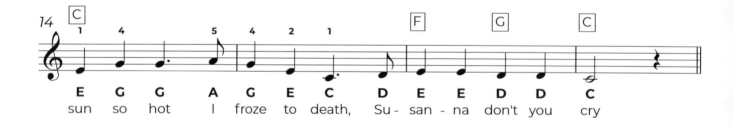

sun so hot I froze to death, Su - san - na don't you cry

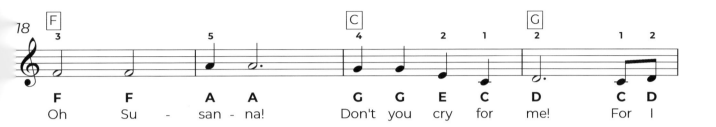

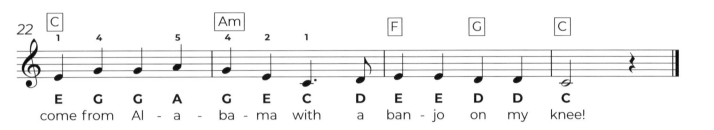

2 I had a dream the other night, when everything was still,
I thought I saw Susanna dear a-comin' down the hill.
A red red rose was in her hand, a tear was in her eye,
I said I come from dixieland, Susanna don't you cry!

Oh Susanna! Oh don't you cry for me!
For I come from Alabama with a banjo on my knee!

3 I soon will be in New Orleans, and then I'll look around,
And when I find Susanna, I'll fall upon the ground.
But if I do not find her, then surely I will die,
And when I'm dead and buried —Susanna, don't you cry.

Oh Susanna! Oh don't you cry for me!
For I come from Alabama with a banjo on my knee!

CAMPTOWN RACES

Stephen C Foster

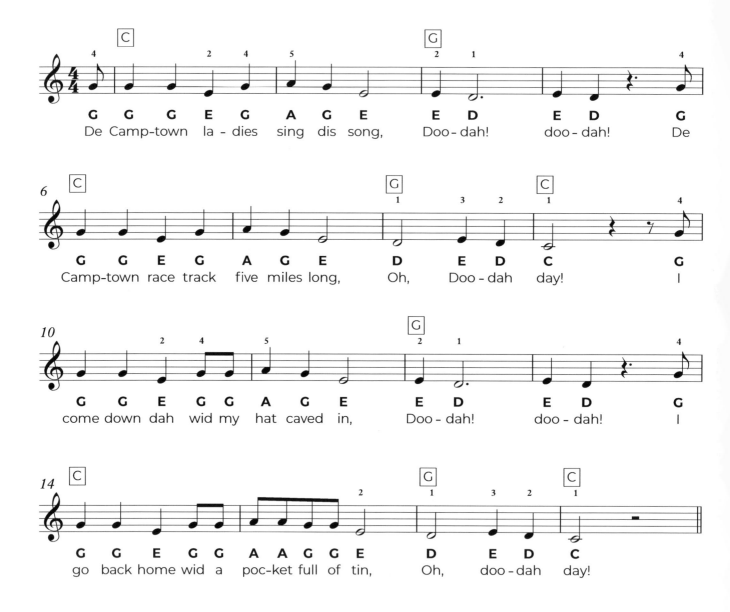

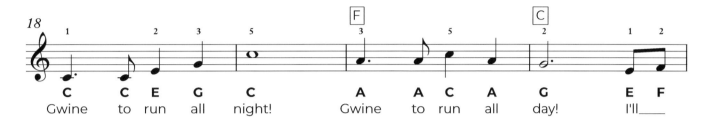

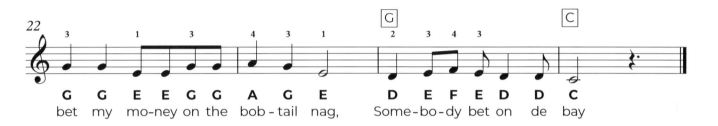

2 De long tail filly and de big black hoss, Doo-dah! doo-dah!
Dey fly de track and dey both cut across, Oh, doo-dah-day!
De blind hoss sticken in a big mud hole, Doo-dah! doo-dah!
Can't touch bottom wid a ten foot pole, Oh, doo-dah-day!
Gwine to run all night...

3 Old muley cow come on to de track, Doo-dah! doo-dah!
De bob-tail fling her ober his back, Oh, doo-dah-day!
Den fly along like a rail-road car, Doo-dah! doo-dah!
Runnin' a race wid a shootin' star, Oh, doo-dah-day!
Gwine to run all night...

4 See dem flyin' on a ten mile heat, Doo-dah doo-dah!
Round de race track, den repeat, Oh, doo-dah-day!
I win my money on de bob-tail nag, Doo-dah! doo-dah!
I keep my money in an old tow-bag, Oh, doo-dah-day!
Gwine to run all night...

God Save the Queen

Traditional

2 Thy choicest gifts in store
On her be pleased to pour,
Long may she reign.
May she defend our laws,
And ever give us cause,
To sing with heart and voice,
God save the Queen.

SWING LOW SWEET CHARIOT

Traditional

2 Swing low, sweet chariot, coming for to carry me home,
Swing low, sweet chariot, coming for to carry me home.

If you get there before I do,
Coming for to carry me home,
Tell all my brothers I'm a coming there too,
Coming for to carry me home.

ROCKIN' ROBIN

Leon René

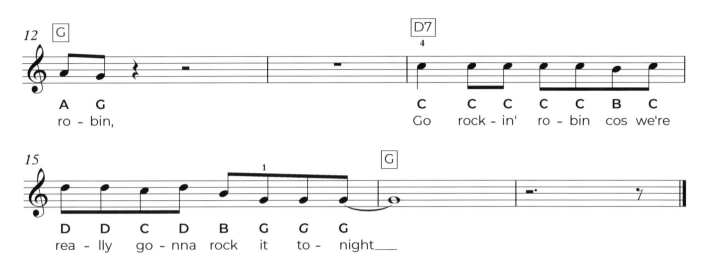

2 Every little swallow, every chick-a-dee,
Every little bird in the tall oak tree,
The wise old owl, the big black crow,
Flappin' their wings signin' "go bird, go."
Rockin' robin...

3 A wordy little raven at the bird's first dance,
Taught him how to do the bop and it was grand,
They started going steady and bless my soul,
He out-bopped the buzzard and the oriole.
Rockin' robin...

4 He rocks in the treetops all day long,
Hoppin' and a-boppin' and singing his song,
All the little birds on Jaybird Street,
Love to hear the robin go tweet-tweet-tweet.
Rockin' robin...

5 Well, the pretty little raven at the bird bandstand,
Taught him how to do the bop and it was grand,
They started going steady and bless my soul,
He out-bopped the buzzard and the oriole.
Rockin' robin...

6 He rocks in the treetops all day long,
Hoppin' and a-boppin' and singing his song,
All the little birds on Jaybird Street,
Love to hear the robin go tweet tweet tweet.
Rockin' robin...

My Bonnie Lies Over The Ocean

Traditional

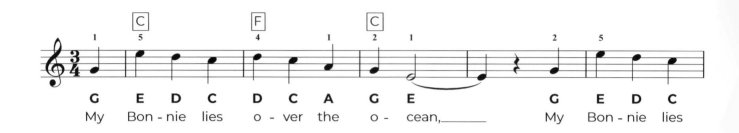

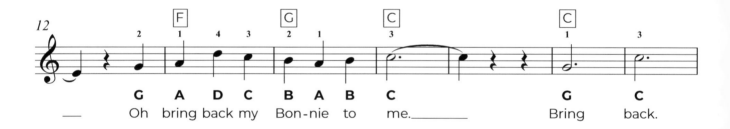

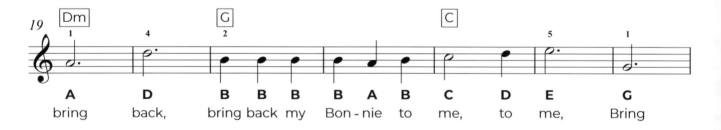

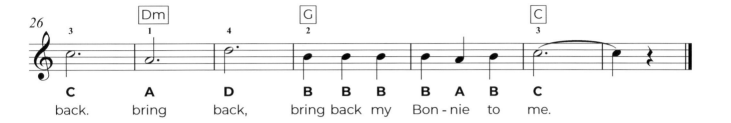

back.   bring   back,   bring back my Bon - nie to me.

2 Last night as I lay on my pillow,
Last night as I lay on my bed,
Last night as I lay on my pillow,
I dreamed that my bonnie was dead.
Bring back, bring back...

3 Oh blow ye the winds o'er the ocean,
And blow ye the winds o'er the sea,
Oh blow ye the winds o'er the ocean,
And bring back my bonnie to me.
Bring back, bring back...

4 The winds have blown over the ocean,
The winds have blown over the sea,
The winds have blown over the ocean,
And brought back my bonnie to me.
Bring back, bring back...

LAVENDER'S BLUE

Traditional

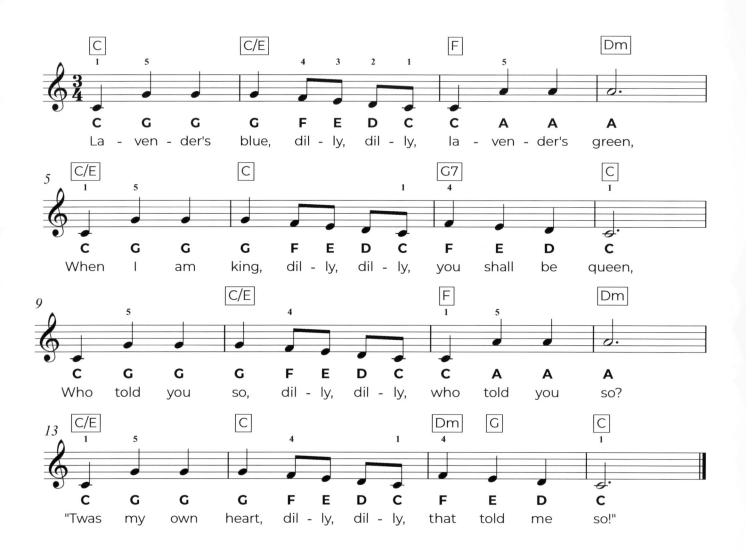

2 Call up your men, dilly dilly, set them to work,
Some with a rake, dilly dilly, some with a fork,
Some to make hay, dilly dilly, some to thresh corn,
Whilst you and I, dilly dilly, keep ourselves warm.

3 If you should die, dilly dilly, as it may hap,
You shall be buried, dilly dilly, under the tap,
Who told you so, dilly dilly, pray tell me why?
That you might drink, dilly dilly, when you are dry

Little Duck

Found a Peanut

Folk song

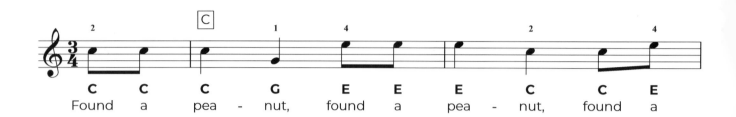

C   C   C   G   E   E   E   C   C   E

Found   a   pea - nut,   found   a   pea - nut,   found   a

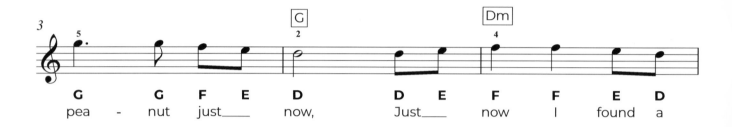

G   G   F   E   D   D   E   F   F   E   D

pea - nut   just____ now,   Just____ now   I   found   a

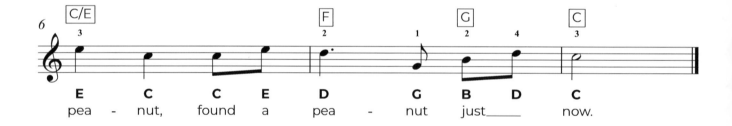

E   C   C   E   D   G   B   D   C

pea - nut,   found   a   pea - nut   just____ now.

2 Cracked it open, cracked it open, cracked it open just now,
I just now cracked it open, cracked it open just now.

3 It was rotten, it was rotten, it was rotten just now,
Just now it was rotten, it was rotten just now .

Oh Christmas Tree

Traditional German Carol

1 O Christmas tree, O Christmas tree,
Much pleasure dost thou bring me!
For ev'ry year the Christmas tree,
Brings to us all both joy and glee.
O Christmas tree, O Christmas tree,
Much pleasure dost thou bring me!

2 O Christmas tree, O Christmas tree,
How lovely are thy branches!
Not only green when summer's here
But in the coldest time of year.
O Christmas tree, O Christmas tree,
How lovely are thy branches!

3 O Christmas tree, O Christmas tree,
How sturdy God hath made thee!
Thou bidd'st us all place faithfully
Our trust in God, unchangingly!
O Christmas tree, O Christmas tree,
How sturdy God hath made thee!

4 O Christmas tree, O Christmas tree,
Thy candles shine out brightly!
Each bough doth hold its tiny light,
That makes each toy to sparkle bright.
O Christmas tree, O Christmas tree,
Thy candles shine out brightly!

THE ANTS GO MARCHING

Traditional

A   A   A   A   G   A   A   A   G   A   A   A   A

down   in   the   ground,   and   up   the   drain,   and   out   in   the   rain.

2 The ants go marching two by two,
hurrah, hurrah,
The ants go marching two by two,
hurrah, hurrah,
The ants go marching two by two,
The little one stops to tie his shoe,
And they all go marching 'round and around,
and down in the ground,
And up the drain and out in the rain.

3 The ants go marching three by three,
hurrah, hurrah,
The ants go marching three by three,
hurrah, hurrah,
The ants go marching three by three,
The little one stops to climb a tree,
And they all go marching 'round and around,
and down in the ground,
And up the drain and out in the rain.

4 The ants go marching four by four,
hurrah, hurrah,
The ants go marching four by four,
hurrah, hurrah,
The ants go marching four by four,
The little one stops to shut the door,
And they all go marching 'round and around,
and down in the ground,
And up the drain and out in the rain.

5 The ants go marching five by five,
hurrah, hurrah,
The ants go marching five by five,
hurrah, hurrah,
The ants go marching five by five,
The little one stops to take a dive,
And they all go marching 'round and around,
and down in the ground,
And up the drain and out in the rain.

6 The ants go marching six by six,
hurrah, hurrah,
The ants go marching six by six, hurrah, hurrah,
The ants go marching six by six,
The little one stops to pick up sticks,
And they all go marching 'round and around,
and down in the ground,
And up the drain and out in the rain.

7 The ants go marching seven by seven,
hurrah, hurrah,
The ants go marching seven by seven,
hurrah, hurrah,
The ants go marching seven by seven,
The little one stops to wave to heaven,
And they all go marching 'round and around,
and down in the ground,
And up the drain and out in the rain.

8 The ants go marching eight by eight,
hurrah, hurrah,
The ants go marching eight by eight,
hurrah, hurrah,
The ants go marching eight by eight,
The little one stops to shut the gate,
And they all go marching 'round and around,
and down in the ground,
And up the drain and out in the rain.

9 The ants go marching nine by nine,
hurrah, hurrah,
The ants go marching nine by nine,
hurrah, hurrah,
The ants go marching nine by nine,
The little one stops to check the time,
And they all go marching 'round and around,
and down in the ground,
And up the drain and out in the rain.

10 The ants go marching ten by ten,
hurrah, hurrah,
The ants go marching ten by ten, hurrah, hurrah,
The ants go marching ten by ten,
The little one stops to say "the end",
And they all go marching 'round and around,
and down in the ground,
And up the drain and out in the rain.

LAND OF THE SILVER BIRCH

American folk song

Dancing and Whirling

Czech Folk Song

THE FIRST NOEL

English Carol

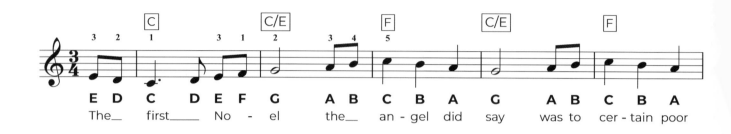

C				C/E		F		C/E		F

E D C D E F G A B C B A G A B C B A

The__ first____ No - el the__ an - gel did say was to cer - tain poor

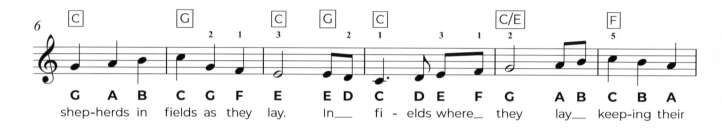

G A B C G F E E D C D E F G A B C B A

shep-herds in fields as they lay. In__ fi - elds where__ they lay__ keep-ing their

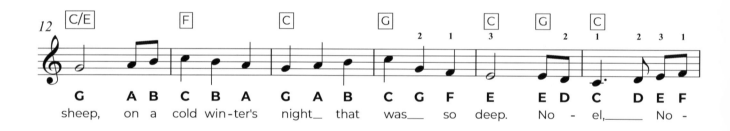

G A B C B A G A B C G F E E D C D E F

sheep, on a cold win-ter's night__ that was__ so deep. No - el,_____ No -

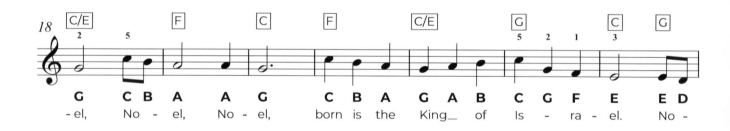

G C B A A G C B A G A B C G F E E D

- el, No - el, No - el, born is the King__ of Is - ra - el. No -

2 They looked up and saw a star,
shining in the east, beyond them far,
and to the earth it gave great light,
and so it continued both day and night.

Noel, noel...

3 And by the light of that same star,
three Wise Men came from country far,
to seek for a king was their intent,
and to follow the star wherever it went.

Noel, noel...

4 This star drew nigh to the northwest,
o'er Bethlehem it took its rest,
and there it did both stop and stay,
right over the place where Jesus lay.

Noel, noel...

5 Then entered in those Wise Men three,
full reverently upon the knee,
and offered there, in his presence,
their gold and myrrh and frankincense.

Noel, noel...

WHAT SHALL WE DO WITH THE DRUNKEN SAILOR

Traditional

E E E E E E E A C E D D D D D D
What shall we do with the drun-ken sai-lor, What shall we do with the

D G B D E E E E E E E F# G A
drun-ken sai-lor, What shall we do with the drun-ken sai-lor,

G E D B A A E E E E A C E
Ear-ly in the morn-ing. Way-hay and up she ri-ses,

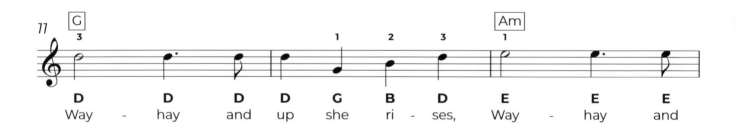

D D D D G B D E E E
Way-hay and up she ri-ses, Way-hay and

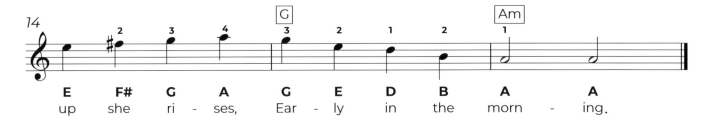

up she ri - ses, Ear - ly in the morn - ing.

2 Shave his belly with a rusty razor,
Shave his belly with a rusty razor,
Shave his belly with a rusty razor,
Early in the morning.
Way hay and up she rises...

3 Put him in a long boat till his sober,
Put him in a long boat till his sober,
Put him in a long boat till his sober,
Early in the morning.
Way hay and up she rises...

4 Stick him in a scupper with a hosepipe bottom,
Stick him in a scupper with a hosepipe bottom,
Stick him in a scupper with a hosepipe bottom,
Early in the morning.
Way hay and up she rises...

5 Put him in the bed with the captains daughter,
Put him in the bed with the captains daughter,
Put him in the bed with the captains daughter,
Early in the morning.
Way hay and up she rises...

6 That's what we do with the drunken sailor,
That's what we do with the drunken sailor,
That's what we do with the drunken sailor,
Early in the morning.
Way hay and up she rises...

The Spanish Ladies

British Naval Song

2   We will rant and we'll roar like true British sailors,
We'll rant and we'll roar all on the salt seas,
Until we strike soundings in the channel of old England,
From Ushant to Scilly is thirty-five leagues.

3   We hove our ship to with the wind from sou'west, boys,
We hove our ship to, deep soundings to take,
'Twas forty-five fathoms, with a white sandy bottom,
So we squared our main yard and up channel did make.

4   We will rant and we'll roar like true British sailors,
We'll rant and we'll roar all on the salt seas,
Until we strike soundings in the channel of old England,
From Ushant to Scilly is thirty-five leagues.

5   The first land we sighted was calléd the Dod-man,
Next Rame Head off Plymouth, Start, Portland and Wight,
We sailed by Beachy, by Fairlight and Dover,
And then we bore up for the South Foreland light.

6   We will rant and we'll roar like true British sailors,
We'll rant and we'll roar all on the salt seas,
Until we strike soundings in the channel of old England,
From Ushant to Scilly is thirty-five leagues.

7   Then the signal was made for the grand fleet to anchor,
And all in the Downs that night for to lie,
Let go your shank painter, let go your cat stopper,
Haul up your clewgarnets, let tacks and sheets fly.

8   We will rant and we'll roar like true British sailors,
We'll rant and we'll roar all on the salt seas,
Until we strike soundings in the channel of old England,
From Ushant to Scilly is thirty-five leagues.

9   Now let ev'ry man drink off his full bumper,
And let ev'ry man drink off his full glass,
We'll drink and be jolly and drown melancholy,
And here's to the health of each true-hearted lass.

10   We will rant and we'll roar like true British sailors,
We'll rant and we'll roar all on the salt seas,
Until we strike soundings in the channel of old England,
From Ushant to Scilly is thirty-five leagues.

JINGLE BELLS

Traditional

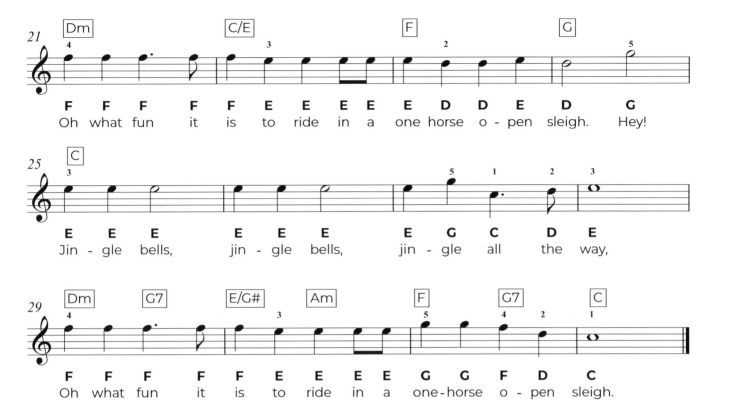

2 Now the ground is white,
Go it while you're young.
Take the girls tonight,
Sing this sleighing song.
Get a bobtailed bay,
Two forty for his speed,
And hitch him to an open sleigh,
And you will take the lead.

Oh, jingle bells, jingle bells,
Jingle all the way.
Oh! what fun it is to ride,
In a one-horse open sleigh, hey!
Jingle bells, jingle bells,
Jingle all the way.
Oh! what fun it is to ride,
In a one-horse open sleigh,
Oh, what fun it is to ride
In one horse open sleigh!

WELLERMAN

Traditional

2 She had not been two weeks from shore,
When down on her a right whale bore,
The captain called all hands and swore,
He'd take that whale in tow.

Soon may the Wellerman come...

3 Before the boat had hit the water,
The whale's tail came up and caught her,
All hands to the side, harpooned and fought her,
When she dived down below.

Soon may the Wellerman come...

4 No line was cut, no whale was freed,
The Captain's mind was not of greed,
But he belonged to the whaleman's creed,
She took the ship in tow.

Soon may the Wellerman come...

5 For forty days, or even more,
The line went slack, then tight once more,
All boats were lost, there were only four,
But still that whale did go.

Soon may the Wellerman come...

6 As far as I've heard, the fight's still on,
The line's not cut and the whale's not gone,
The Wellerman makes his regular call,
To encourage the Captain, crew, and all.

Soon may the Wellerman come...

Down in the Valley

Jimmie Tarlton

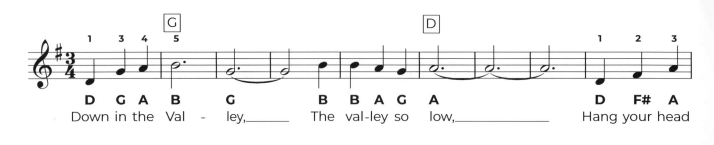

D G A B G B B A G A D F# A

Down in the Val - ley,_____ The val-ley so low,_____ Hang your head

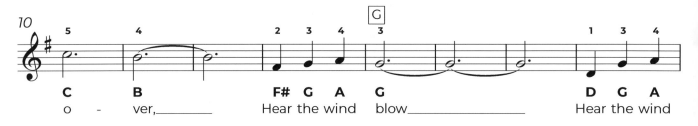

C B F# G A G D G A

o - ver,_____ Hear the wind blow_____ Hear the wind

B G B A G A

blow dear,_____ Hear the wind blow,_____

D F# A C B F# G A G

Hang your head o - ver,_____ Hear the wind blow_____

2 Roses love sunshine,
Violets love dew,
Angels in heaven,
Know I love you,
Know I love you dear,
Know I love you,
Angels in heaven,
Know I love you.

3 If you don't love me,
Love whom you please,
Throw your arms 'round me,
Give my heart ease,
Give my heart ease love,
Give my heart ease,
Throw your arms round me,
Give my heart ease.

4 Build me a castle,
Forty feet high,
So I can see him,
As he rides by,
As he rides by love,
As he rides by,
So I can see him,
As he rides by.

5 Write me a letter,
Send it by mail,
Send it in care of,
Birmingham jail,
Birmingham jail love,
Birmingham jail,
Send it in care of,
Birmingham jail.

SAKURA SAKURA

Traditional Japanese

2 Sakura, Sakura, blossoms waving in the breeze,
Yoshina, the cherry land,
Tatsuta, the maple trees,
Karasaki, pine tree grand,
Sakura, Sakura,
let all come singing.

MAIRI'S WEDDING

Traditional

Step we gai - ly on we go, Heel for heel and toe for toe,__

Arm in arm and row on row, all for Mai - ri's wed - ding.

O - ver hill - ways up and down, Myr - tle green and brack - en brown,__

Past the shiel - dings through the town, All for Mai - ri's wed - ding.

2 Red her cheeks as rowans are,
Bright her eye as any star,
Fairest o' them a' by far,
Is our darling Mairi.
Plenty herring, plenty meal,
Plenty peat to fill her creel,
Plenty bonnie bairns as weel,
That's the toast for Mairi.

OH YES

German Folk Song

GOING UP ON THE MOUNTAIN

Traditional

Go - in' up on the moun-tain to raise a crop of cane, To make a bar-rel of las - ses, To sweet-en old Li - za Jane. It's a bye, bye, my dar - ling girl, Bye, bye, I'm gone, Bye, bye, my dar - ling girl, with the gol - den slip - pers on.

2 I used to ride the old gray horse,
But now I ride the roan,
You may court your own true love,
But you'd better leave mine alone.
It's a bye, bye...

3 Meat's on the goose's foot,
The marrow's in the bone,
Every girl that's here tonight

Is sweeter than honeycomb.
It's a bye, bye...

4 I used to make my living
By railroad and steam,
But now I make my living
By high low Jack, and the game.
It's a bye, bye...

COCKLES AND MUSSELS

Traditional Irish

In Du-blin's fair ci-ty, Where the girls are so pret-ty, I

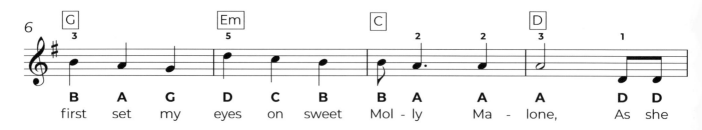

first set my eyes on sweet Mol-ly Ma-lone, As she

wheeled her wheel bar-row, Through streets broad and nar-row, Cry-ing

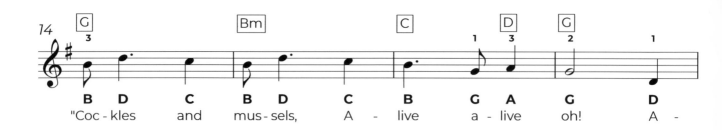

"Coc-kles and mus-sels, A - live a-live oh! A -

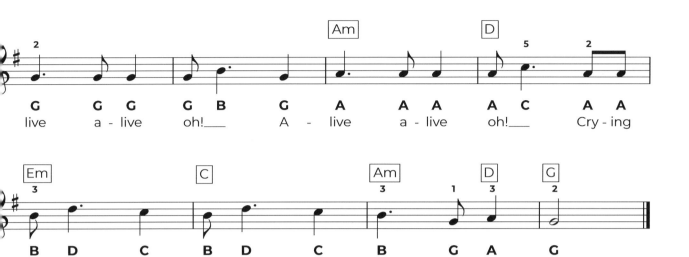

2 She was a fishmonger,
But sure 'twas no wonder,
For so were her father and mother before,
And they each wheel'd their barrow,
Through streets broad and narrow,
Crying "Cockles and mussels alive, alive oh!"

"Alive, alive, oh..."

3 She died of a fever,
And no one could save her,
And that was the end of sweet Molly Malone,
But her ghost wheels her barrow,
Through streets broad and narrow,
Crying, "Cockles and mussels, alive, alive, oh!"

"Alive, alive, oh..."

Down in the River to Pray

Traditional

2   As I went down in the river to pray,
Studying about that good old way,
And who shall wear the robe and crown?
Good Lord, show me the way.

O brothers let's go down,
Let's go down, come on down,
Come on brothers, let's go down,
Down in the river to pray.

3   As I went down in the river to pray,
Studying about that good old way,
And who shall wear the starry crown?
Good Lord, show me the way.

O fathers let's go down,
Let's go down, come on down,
O fathers let's go down,
Down in the river to pray.

4   As I went down in the river to pray,
Studying about that good old way,
And who shall wear the robe and cr,own?
Good Lord, show me the way.

O mothers let's go down,
Come on down, don't you wanna go down?
Come on mothers, let's go down,
Down in the river to pray.

5   As I went down in the river to pray,
Studying about that good old way,
And who shall wear the starry crown?
Good Lord, show me the way.

O sinners, let's go down,
Let's go down, come on down,
O sinners, let's go down,
Down in the river to pray.

6   As I went down in the river to pray,
Studying about that good old way,
And who shall wear the robe and crown?
Good Lord, show me the way.

HOME SWEET HOME

Traditional

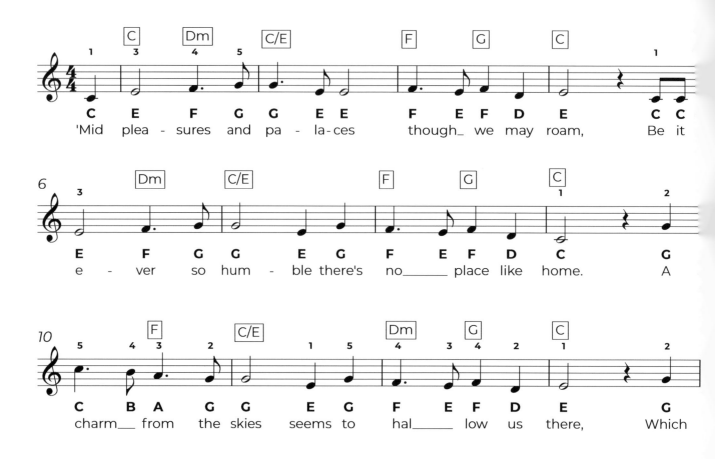

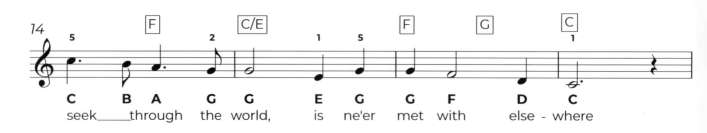

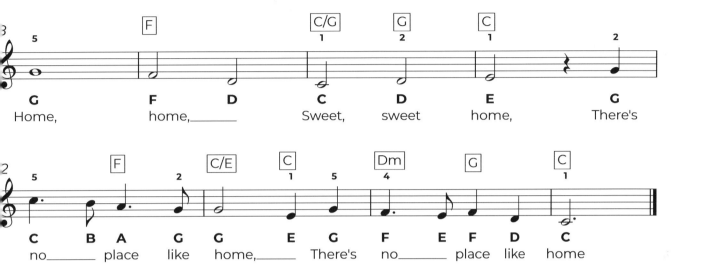

2 An exile from home splendor dazzles in vain,
Oh give me my lowly thatched cottage again,
The birds singing gaily that came at my call,
And gave me the peace of mind dearer than all,
Home, home, sweet, sweet home,
There's no place like home, there's no place like home.

Home, Home,
Sweet, sweet home,
There's no place like home,
There's no place like home.

NELLY BLY

Stephen Foster

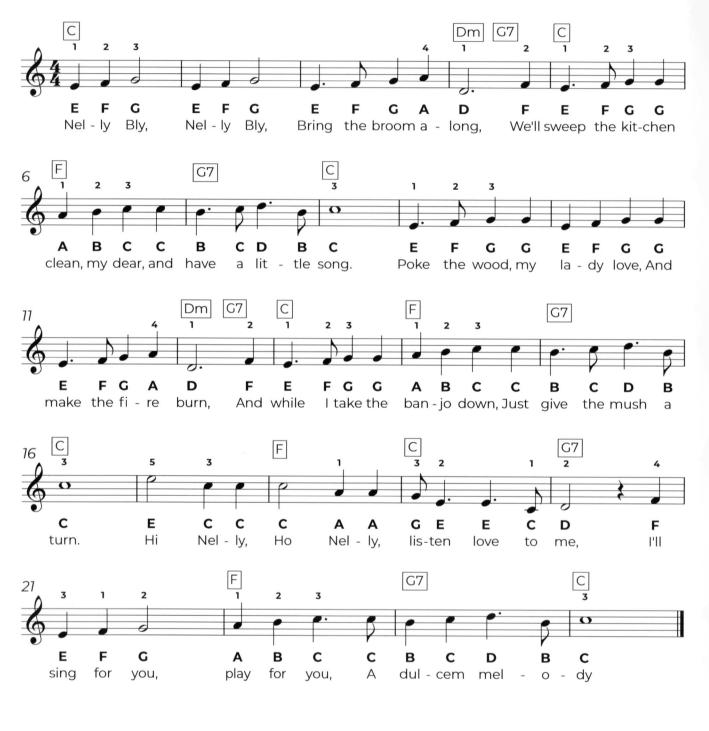

2 Nelly Bly has a voice like a turtle dove,
I hear it in the meadow and I hear it in the grove,
Nelly Bly has a heart warm as a cup of tea,
And bigger than the sweet potatoes down in Tennessee.

Hi, Nelly, Ho Nelly...

3 Nelly Bly shuts her eye when she goes to sleep,
When she wakens up again her eyeballs start to peep,
The way she walks, she lifts her foot, and then she bumps it down,
And when it lights, there's music there, in that part of the town.

Hi, Nelly, Ho Nelly...

4 Nelly Bly! Nelly Bly! Never, never sigh,
Never bring the tear drop to the corner of your eye,
For the pie is made of pumpkins, and the mush is made of corn,
And there's corn and pumpkins plenty, love, a-lyin' in the barn.

Hi, Nelly, Ho Nelly...

Danny Boy

Traditional Irish

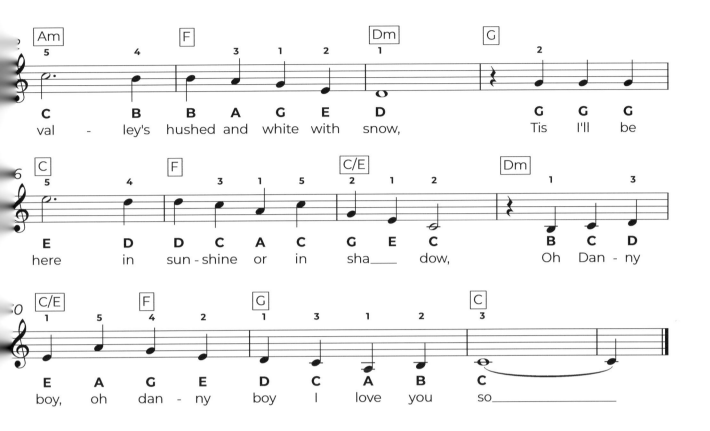

2 But when ye come, and all the flowers are dying,
If I am dead, as dead I well may be,
Ye'll come and find the place where I am lying,
And kneel and say an Ave there for me.
And I shall hear, though soft you tread above me,
And all my grave will warmer, sweeter be,
For you will bend and tell me that you love me,
And I shall sleep in peace until you come to me.

MAMA PAQUITA

Brazilian Folk Song

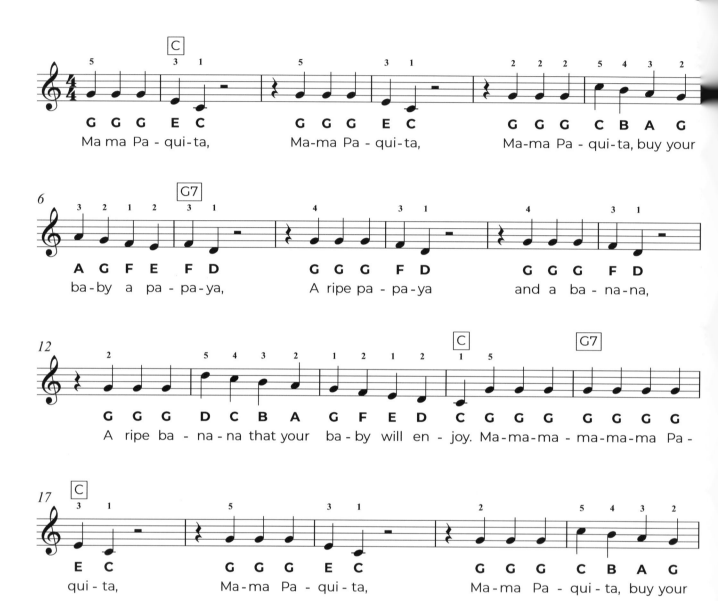

ba - by a pa - pa - ya, A ripe pa - pa - ya And a ba -

na - na, Let's go to Car - ni - val and dance the night a - way.

2 Mama Paquita, Mama Paquita,
Mama Paquita, buy your baby some pajamas,
Some new pajamas, a yellow blanket,
A yellow blanket that your baby will enjoy.
Ma-ma-ma-ma Mama Paquita, Mama Paquita,
Mama Paquita, buy your baby some pajamas,
Some new pajamas, a yellow blanket,
Let's go to Carnival to dance the night away.

COTTON EYED JOE

Traditional

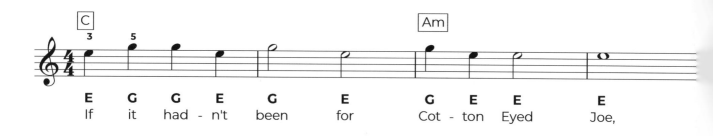

E G G E G E G E E E
If it had - n't been for Cot - ton Eyed Joe,

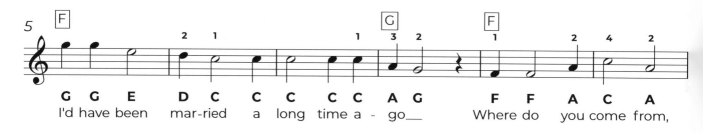

G G E D C C C C A G F F A C A
I'd have been mar-ried a long time a - go___ Where do you come from,

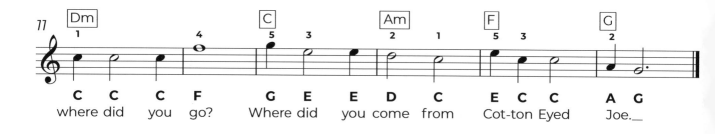

C C C F G E E D C E C C A G
where did you go? Where did you come from Cot-ton Eyed Joe.___

DING DONG BELL

Traditional English

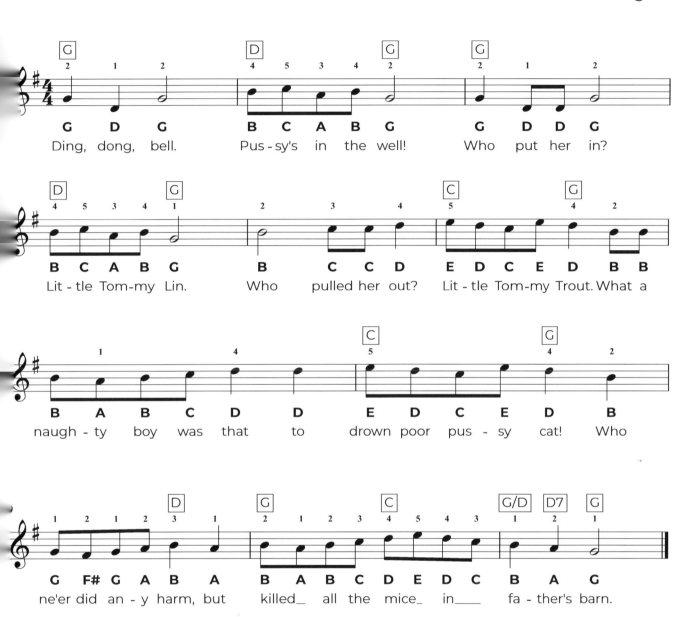

THE COCKROACH

Mexican Folk Song

The lit-tle cock-roach, the lit-tle cock-roach, All she want-ed was to dance, She doesn't mind that a leg is mis-sing, And she would ne-ver miss the chance. The lit-tle cock-roach, the lit-tle cock-roach, All she want-ed was to dance, She doesn't mind that a leg is mis-sing, And she would ne-ver miss the chance. In the

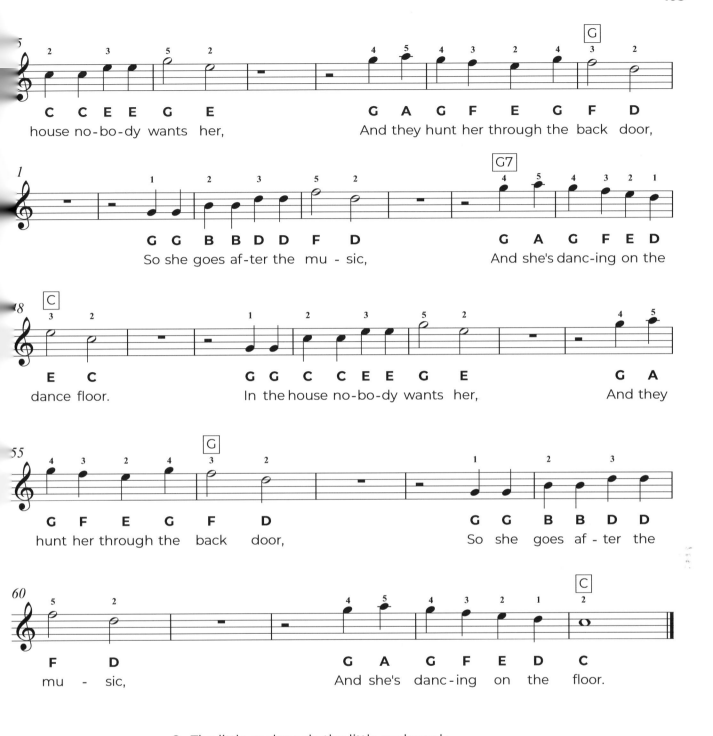

2 The little cockroach, the little cockroach,
All she wanted was to dance,
She doesn't mind that
A leg is missing,
She would never miss the chance.
She won't stay where they don't want her,
There are better things to ask for.
Now the music seems to charm her
As she's dancing on the dance floor.

FIVE GREY ELEPHANTS

Traditional

E E E C D   C C C   D D D C C
One grey e - le - phant ba - lan - cing   step by step on a

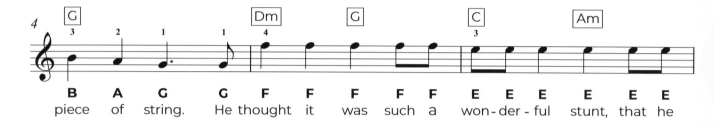

B A G G F F F F F   E E E E E E
piece of string. He thought it was such a won-der-ful stunt, that he

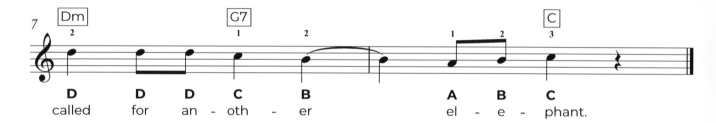

D D D C B   A B C
called for an - oth - er   el - e - phant.

1 Two grey elephants balancing,
Step by step on a piece of string,
Thought it was such a wonderful stunt,
That they called for another elephant.

2 Three grey elephants balancing,
Step by step on a piece of string,
Thought it was such a wonderful stunt,
That they called for another elephant.

3 Four grey elephants balancing,
Step by step on a piece of string,
Thought it was such a wonderful stunt,
That they called for another elephant.

4 Five grey elephants balancing,
Step by step on a piece of string,
All of a sudden the piece of string broke,
And down came all the elephant folk.

Rock-a-Bye Baby

Traditional

The Wild Rover

Traditional Irish

C C D C A G E E D E F — E F
I've been a wild ro - ver for ma - ny a year,_____ And I've

G E G F D B G E D C — C
spent all my mo - ney on whis - key and beer,_____ But

C D C A G E E D E F — E F
now I'm re - turn - ing with gold in great store,_____ And I

G E G F D B G E D C B C
swear I will play the wild ro - ver no more, And it's

D D B G — E E
no, nay, ne - ver,_____ No, nay,

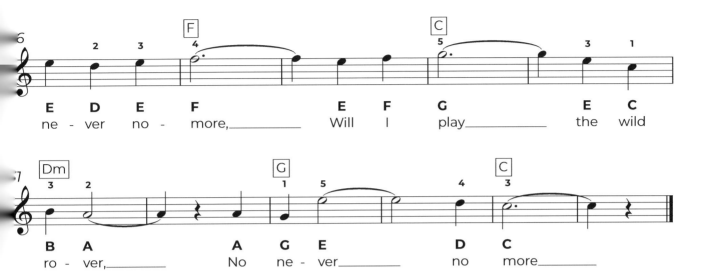

2   I went into an alehouse that I used to frequent,
And I told the landlady me money was spent,
I asked her for credit, but she answered me nay,
Such a customer as you I can get any day.

And it's no, nay, never...

3   Then I took from me pocket, a handful of gold,
And on the round table it glittered and rolled,
Well the landlady smiled as she served me the best,
What I told you before sure it was only in jest.

And it's no, nay, never...

4   I'll go back to my parents, confess what I've done,
And I'll ask them to pardon their prodigal son,
And, when they forgive me as oft times before,
Then I swear I will play the wild rover no more.

And it's no, nay, never...

Amazing Grace

Lyrics: John Newton

2 Shout, shout for glory,
Shout, shout aloud for glory,
Brother, sister, mourner,
All shout glory hallelujah.

Pack Up Your Troubles in your Old Kit Bag

Lyrics: George Henry Powell
Music: Felix Powell

G G A G F E F G E E D C A G
Pack up your trou-bles in your old kit bag and smile, smile smile,

G G A G F E F G E C D A B C D
Don't let your joy and lagh-ter hear the snag, Smile boys, that's the style.

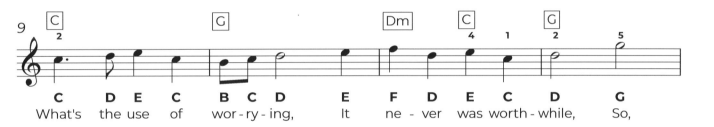

C D E C B C D E F D E C D G
What's the use of wor-ry-ing, It ne-ver was worth-while, So,

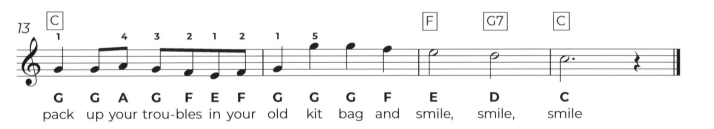

G G A G F E F G G G F E D C
pack up your trou-bles in your old kit bag and smile, smile, smile

Home on the Range

Lyrics: Brewster M Higley
Music: Daniel E Kelley

C	**C**	**C**	**C**	**B**	**C**	**D**	**G**
deer	and	the	an	- te -	lope	play,_____	Where

G	**C**	**D**	**E**	**C**	**B**	**A**	**F**	**F**	**F**	**F**	**F**
sel -	dom	is	heard	a	dis -	cour -	a -	ging	word,	And the

E	**D**	**C**	**B**	**C**	**D**	**C**
skies	are	not	clou -	dy	all	day_____

2 Where the air is so pure, the zephyrs so free,
The breezes so balmy and light,
That I would not exchange my home on the range,
For all of the cities so bright.

Home, home on the range...

3 The red man was pressed from this part of the West,
He's likely no more to return,
To the banks of Red River where seldom if ever,
Their flickering camp-fires burn.

Home, home on the range...

4 How often at night when the heavens are bright,
With the light from the glittering stars,
Have I stood here amazed and asked as I gazed,
If their glory exceeds that of ours.

Home, home on the range...

5 Oh, I love these wild flowers in this dear land of ours,
The curlew I love to hear scream,
And I love the white rocks and the antelope flocks,
That graze on the mountain-tops green.

Home, home on the range...

6 Oh, give me a land where the bright diamond sand,
Flows leisurely down the stream,
Where the graceful white swan goes gliding along,
Like a maid in a heavenly dream.

Home, home on the range...

7 Then I would not exchange my home on the range,
Where the deer and the antelope play,
Where seldom is heard a discouraging word,
And the skies are not cloudy all day.

Home, home on the range...

Santa Lucia

Neopolitan Folk Song

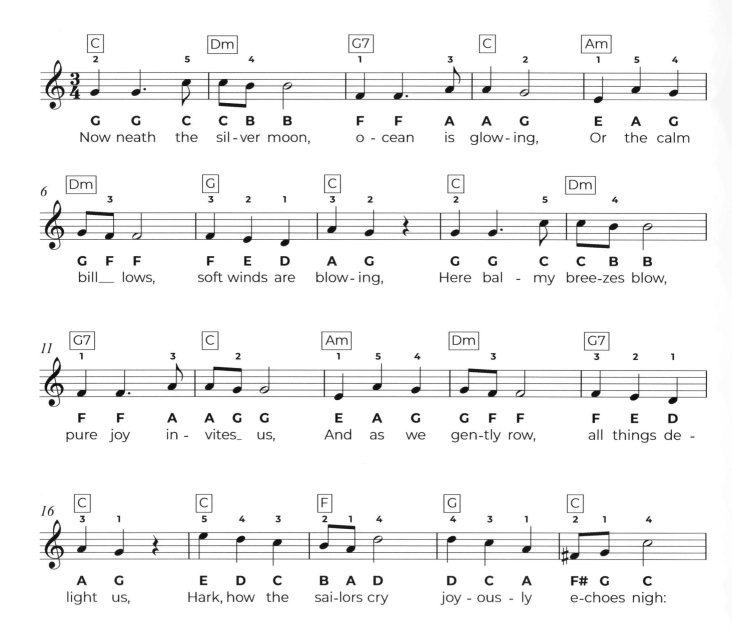

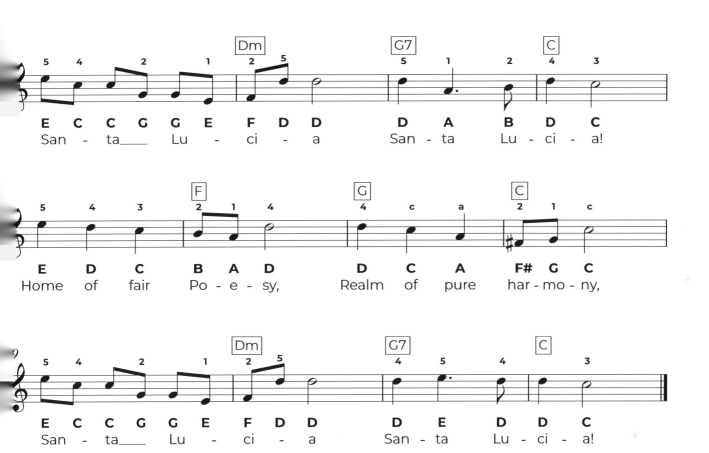

2 When o'er the waters light winds are playing,
Thy spell can soothe us, all care allaying.
To thee sweet Napoli, what charms are given,
Where smiles creation, toil blest by heaven.

Hark, how the sailor's cry joyously echoes nigh:
Santa Lucia, Santa Lucia!
Home of fair Poesy, realm of pure harmony,
Santa Lucia, Santa Lucia!

ALL ME ROCK

Traditional Jamaica

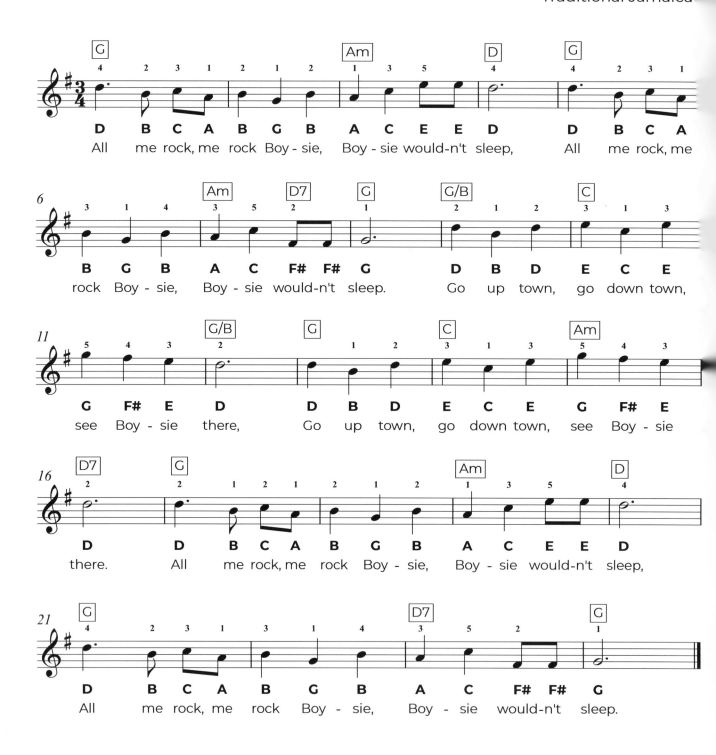

Blue Bells of Scotland

Scottish Folk Song

2 Oh where, tell me where, did your Highland laddie dwell?
Oh where, tell me where, did your Highland laddie dwell?
He dwelt in Bonnie Scotland, where blooms the sweet bluebell,
And it's oh, in my heart I love my laddie well

3 Oh what, tell me what, does your Highland laddie wear?
Oh what, tell me what, does your Highland laddie wear?

A bonnet with a lofty plume, and on his breast a plaid,
And it's oh, in my heart I lo'ed my Highland lad

4 Oh what, tell me what, if your Highland laddie is slain?
Oh what, tell me what, if your Highland laddie is slain?
Oh no, true love will be his guard and bring him safe again,
For it's oh, my heart would break if my Highland lad were slain.

RAIN OR SHINE

American folk song

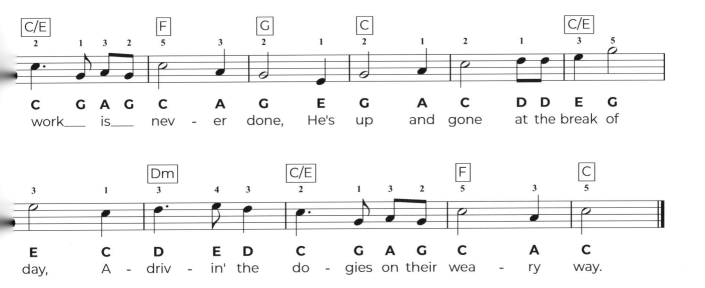

work___ is___ nev - er done, He's up and gone at the break of
day, A - driv - in' the do - gies on their wea - ry way.

2 It's rain or shine, sleet or snow,
Me and my Doney gal are on the go,
Yes, rain or shine, sleet or snow,
Me and my Doney gal are bound to go.

A cowboy's life is a dreary thing,
For it's rope and brand and ride and sing,
Yes, day or night in the rain or hail,
He'll stay with his dogies out on the trail.

3 It's rain or shine, sleet or snow,
Me and my Doney gal are on the go,
Yes, rain or shine, sleet or snow,
Me and my Doney gal are bound to go.

We whoop at the sun and yell through the hail
But we drive the poor dogies down the trail,
And we'll laugh at the storms, the sleet and snow,
When we reach the little town of San Antonio.

THE IRISH ROVER

Traditiona

twen-ty-se-ven masts, And they called her the I - rish Ro - ver.

2 We had one million bags of the best Sligo rags,
We had two million barrels of bone,
We had three million bails of old nanny goats' tails,
We had four million barrels of stone,
We had five million dogs and six million hogs,
Seven million barrels of Porter,
We had eight million bails of old blind horses hides,
In the hold of the Irish Rover.

3 There was awl Mickey Coote who played hard on his flute,
When the ladies lined up for a set,
He was tootin' with skill for each sparkling quadrille,
Though the dancers were fluther'd and bet,
With his smart witty talk, he was cock of the walk,
And he rolled the dames under and over,
They all knew at a glance when he took up his stance,
That he sailed in The Irish Rover.

4 There was Barney McGee from the banks of the Lee,
There was Hogan from County Tyrone,
There was Johnny McGurk who was scared stiff of work,
And a man from Westmeath called Malone,

There was Slugger O'Toole who was drunk as a rule,
And fighting Bill Tracy from Dover,
And your man, Mick MacCann from the banks of the Bann,
Was the skipper of the Irish Rover.

5 For a sailor it's always a bother in life,
It's so lonesome by night and by day,
And he longs for the shore and a pretty young whore,
Who will melt all his troubles away,
All the noise and the rout swillin' poteen and stout,
For him soon is done and over,
Of the love of a maid, he is never afraid,
An old salt from the Irish Rover.

6 We had sailed seven years when the measles broke out,
And the ship had lost its way in the fog,
And that whale of a crew was reduced down to two,
Just myself and the Captain's old dog,
Then the ship struck a rock, oh Lord! What a shock,
The bulkhead was turned right over
Turned nine times around and the poor ol,d dog was drowned,
And I'm the last of The Irish Rover.

WHISKEY IN THE JAR

Traditional Irish

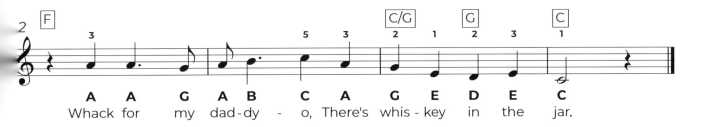

2 I counted out his money and it made a pretty penny,
I put it in me pocket and I took it home to Jenny,
She sighed and she swore that she never would deceive me,
But the devil take the women for they never can be easy.

Mush-a ring dum-a do dum-a da...

3 I went up to my chamber, all for to take a slumber,
I dreamt of gold and jewels and for sure 't was no wonder,
But Jenny drew me charges and she filled them up with water,
Then sent for captain Farrell to be ready for the slaughter.

Mush-a ring dum-a do dum-a da...

4 'Twas was early in the morning, just before I rose to travel,
Up comes a band of footmen and likewise Captain Farrell,
I first produced me pistol for she stole away me rapier,
I couldn't shoot the water, so a prisoner I was taken.

Mush-a ring dum-a do dum-a da...

5 Now there's some take delight in the carriages a-rollin',
And others take delight in the hurling and the bowling,
But I take delight in the juice of the barley,
And courting pretty fair maids in the morning bright and early.

Mush-a ring dum-a do dum-a da...

6 If anyone can aid me 't is my brother in the army,
If I can find his station in Cork or in Killarney,
And if he'll go with me, we'll go rovin' through Killkenny,
And I'm sure he'll treat me better than my own a-sporting Jenny.

Mush-a ring dum-a do dum-a da...

Scarborough Fair

Traditional English

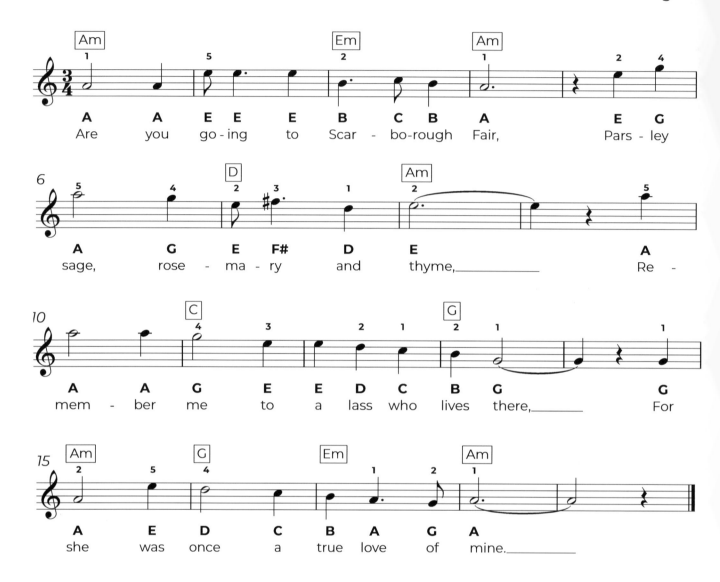

2 And tell her to make me a cambric shirt,
Savoury sage, rosemary, and thyme,
Without any seam or needlework,
And then she shall be a true love of mine.

3 And tell her to wash it in yonder dry well,
Savoury sage, rosemary, and thyme,
Where no water sprung, nor a drop of rain fell,
And then she shall be a true love of mine.

PAT-A-PAN

Bernard de La Monnoye

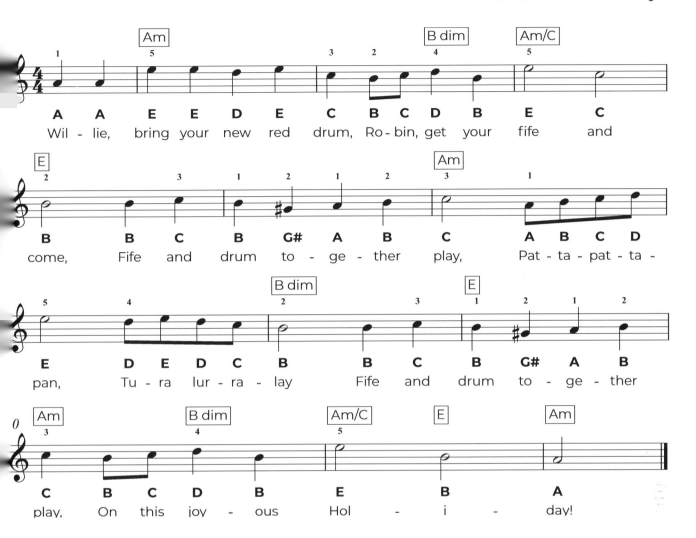

Wil - lie, bring your new red drum, Ro - bin, get your fife and come, Fife and drum to - ge - ther play, Pat - ta - pat - ta - pan, Tu - ra lur - ra - lay Fife and drum to - ge - ther play, On this joy - ous Hol - i - day!

2 When the men of olden days,
To the King of Kings gave praise,
On the fife and drum did play,
Patta-patta-pan, turra-lurra-lay,
On the fife and drum did play,
So their hearts were glad and gay.

3 There is music in the air,
You can hear it everywhere,
Fife and drum together play,

Patta-patta-pan, turra-lurra-lay,
Fife and drum together play,
On this joyous Holiday.

4 God and man today become,
More in tune than fife and drum,
Fife and drum together play,
Patta-patta-pan, turra-lurra-lay,
Fife and drum together play,
On this joyous Holiday.

SHE MOVED THROUGH THE FAIR

Traditional Irish

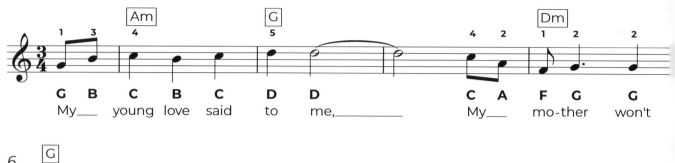

My— young love said to me,_____ My— mo-ther won't

mind,_____ And my fa - ther won't slight you for

lack___ of kind,_____ And she stepped a - way

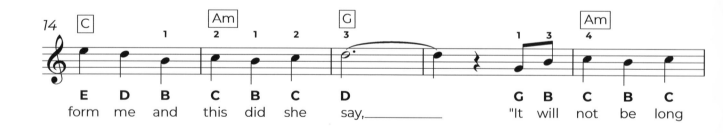

form me and this did she say,_____ "It will not be long

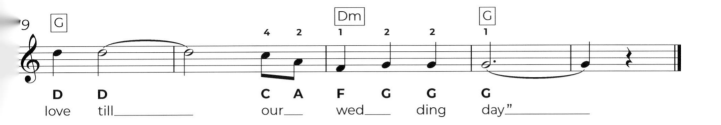

love   till_____   our___   wed___   ding   day"_____

2 And she went away from me,
and moved through the fair,
And fondly I watched her,
move here, and move there,
And then she went onward,
just one star awake,
Like the swan in the evening,
moves over the lake.

3 Last night she came to me,
my dead love came in,
So softly she came,
that her feet made no din,
And she laid her hand on me,
and this she did say,
"Oh, it will not be long, love,
till our wedding-day".

Waltzing Matilda

Lyrics: Banjo Paterson
Music: Traditional

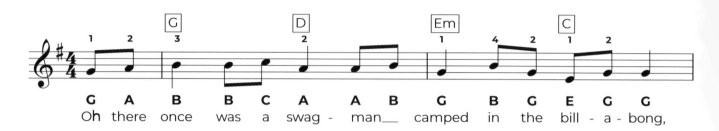

G A B | B C A A B | G B G E G G
Oh there once was a swag - man__ camped in the bill - a - bong,

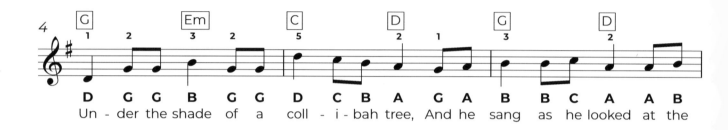

D G G B | G G D | C B A | G A B | B C A A B
Un - der the shade of a coll - i - bah tree, And he sang as he looked at the

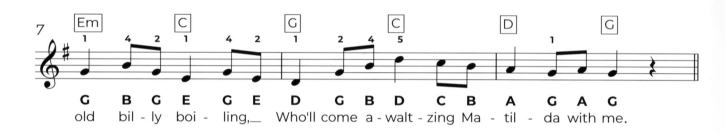

G B G E | G E D | G B D | C B A | G A G
old bil - ly boi - ling,__ Who'll come a - walt - zing Ma - til - da with me.

D D D D | B | G G G F# E | D D D E D D
Walt - zing Ma - til - da, walt - zing Ma - til - da, You'll come a - walt - zing Ma -

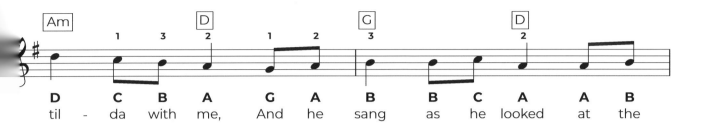

Am   1   3 D 2   1   2 G 3   D 2

D   C   B   A   G   A   B   B   C   A   A   B

til - da with me, And he sang as he looked at the

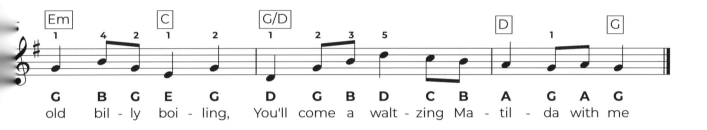

Em 1   4 2 C 1   2 G/D 1   2 3 5   D   1   G

G   B   G   E   G   D   G   B   D   C   B   A   G   A   G

old bil - ly boi - ling, You'll come a walt - zing Ma - til - da with me

2 Down came a jumbuck to drink at that billabong,
Up jumped the swagman and grabbed him with glee,
And he sang as he shoved[N 1] that jumbuck in his tucker bag,
You'll come a-waltzing Matilda, with me.

Waltzing Matilda, waltzing Matilda...

3 Up rode the squatter, mounted on his thoroughbred,
Down came the troopers, one, two, and three,
Whose is that jumbuck you've got in your tucker bag?
You'll come a-waltzing Matilda, with me.

Waltzing Matilda, waltzing Matilda...

4 Up jumped the swagman and sprang into the billabong,
"You'll never catch me alive!" said he,
And his ghost may be heard as you pass by that billabong:
You'll come a-waltzing Matilda, with me.

Waltzing Matilda, waltzing Matilda...

HOUSE OF THE RISING SUN

Traditional

2 Well mothers tell your children,
Not to do what I have done,
While you spend your life in sin and misery,
In the House of the Rising Sun.

3 Well there is a house in New Orleans,
They call the Rising Sun,
Well It's been the ruin of many a poor boy,
And God I know I'm one.

AULD LANG SYNE

Scottish folk song
Lyrics: Thomas Burns

2 And surely you'll buy your pint cup!
And surely I'll buy mine!
And we'll take a cup o' kindness yet,
for auld lang syne.
For auld lang syne...

3 We two have run about the hills,
And picked the daisies fine,
But we've wandered many a weary foot,
since auld lang syne.
For auld lang syne...

4 We two have paddled in the stream,
From morning sun till dine;
But seas between us broad have roared
since auld lang syne.
For auld lang syne...

5 And there's a hand my trusty friend!
And give me a hand o' thine!
And we'll take a right good-will draught,
for auld lang syne.
For auld lang syne...

God Rest Ye Merry Gentlemen

Traditional

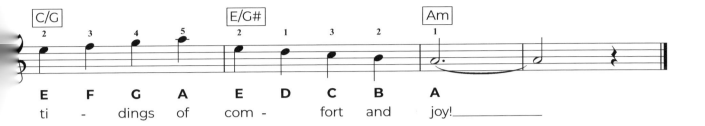

C/G   E/G#   Am

2 | 3 | 4 | 5 | 2 | 1 | 3 | 2 | 1

E   F   G   A   E   D   C   B   A

ti - dings of com - fort and joy!_____

2 God rest ye merry gentlemen,
Let nothing you dismay,
Remember Christ our Savior,
Was born on Christmas Day,
To save us all from Satan's pow'r,
When we were gone astray,
Oh tidings of comfort and joy,
Comfort and joy,
Oh tidings of comfort and joy.

3 In Bethlehem, in Israel,
This blessed Babe was born,
And laid within a manger,
Upon this blessed morn,
The which His Mother Mary,
Did nothing take in scorn,
Oh tidings of comfort and joy,
Comfort and joy,
Oh tidings of comfort and joy.

4 Fear not then, said the Angel,
Let nothing you affright,
This day is born a Savior,
Of a pure Virgin bright,
To free all those who trust in Him,
From Satan's pow'r and might,
Oh tidings of comfort and joy,
Comfort and joy,
Oh tidings of comfort and joy.

5 God rest ye merry gentlemen,
Let nothing you dismay,
Remember Christ our Savior,
Was born on Christmas Day,
To save us all from Satan's pow'r,
When we were gone astray,
Oh tidings of comfort and joy,
Comfort and joy,
Oh tidings of comfort and joy.

The Coventry Carol

Traditional

2 O sisters too, how may we do,
For to preserve this day,
This poor youngling for whom we sing,
"Bye bye, lully, lullay?"

3 Herod the king, in his raging,
Chargèd he hath this day,
His men of might in his own sight,
All young children to slay.

4 That woe is me, poor child, for thee,
And ever mourn and may,
For thy parting neither say nor sing,
"Bye bye, lully, lullay."

DOWN BY THE BAY

Traditional

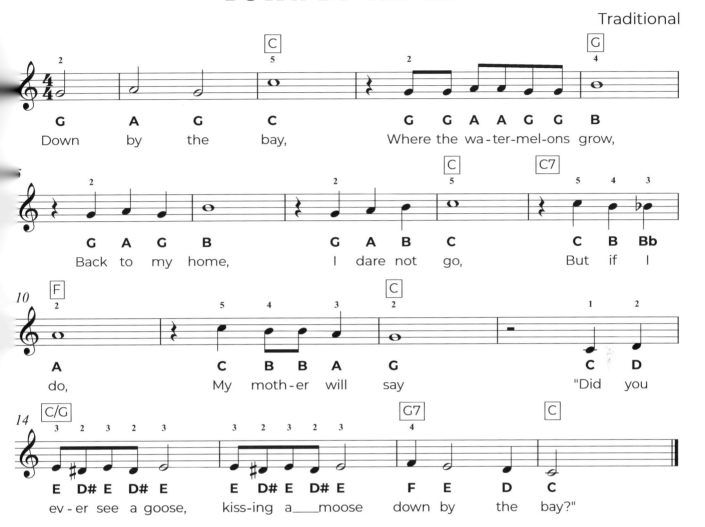

"Did you ever see a llama,
Eating his pajamas?
Down by the bay!"

"Did you ever see a bear,
Combing his hair?
Down by the bay!"

"Did you ever see a whale,
With a polka dot tail?
Down by the bay!"

"Did you ever see a fly,
Wearing a tie?
Down by the bay!"

"Did you ever see a bee,
With a sunburned knee?
Down by the bay!"

"Did you ever see a pig,
Wearing a wig?
Down by the bay!"

"Did you ever have a time,
When you couldn't make a rhyme?
Down by the bay!"

O Little Town Of Bethlehem

Text: Phillips Brooks
Music: Lewis Redner

2 For Christ is born of Mary, and gathered all above,
While mortals sleep the angels keep their watch of wondering love,
Oh morning stars together, proclaim thy holy birth,
And praises sing to God the king, and peace to men on earth.

3 Oh little town of Bethlehem, how still we see thee lie,
Above thy deep and dreamless sleep the silent stars go by,
Yet in thy dark streets shineth, the everlasting light,
The hopes and fears of all the years are met in thee tonight.

DECK THE HALLS

Traditional

2 See the blazing Yule before us
Fa-la-la-la-la, la-la-la-la
Strike the harp and join the chorus
Fa-la-la-la-la, la-la-la-la
Follow me in merry measure
Fa-la-la, la-la-la, la-la-la
While I tell of Yule-tide treasure
Fa-la-la-la-la, la-la-la-la

3 Fast away the old year passes
Fa-la-la-la-la, la-la-la-la
Hail the new year, lads and lasses
Fa-la-la-la-la, la-la-la-la
Sing we joyous, all together
Fa-la-la, la-la-la, la-la-la
Heedless of the wind and weather
Fa-la-la-la-la, la-la-la-la

CAROL OF THE BELLS

Mykola Leontovych

C B C A   C B C A   C B C A   C B C A
Hark! how the bells, sweet sil - ver bells, all seem to say: "Throw cares a - way,

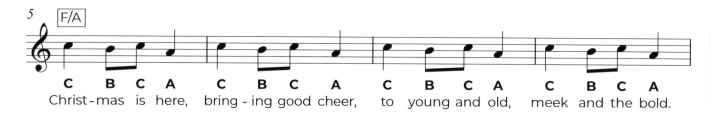

C B C A   C B C A   C B C A   C B C A
Christ-mas is here, bring - ing good cheer, to young and old, meek and the bold.

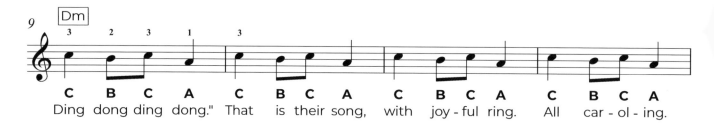

C B C A   C B C A   C B C A   C B C A
Ding dong ding dong." That is their song, with joy - ful ring. All car - ol - ing.

C B C A   C B C A   C B C A   C B C A
One seems to hear, words of good cheer, from ev' - ry where fil - ling the air,

C B C A   C B C A   C B C A   C B C A
Oh how they pound, rai - sing the sound, O'er hill and dale, tel - ling their tale.

Star of the County Down

Traditional Irish

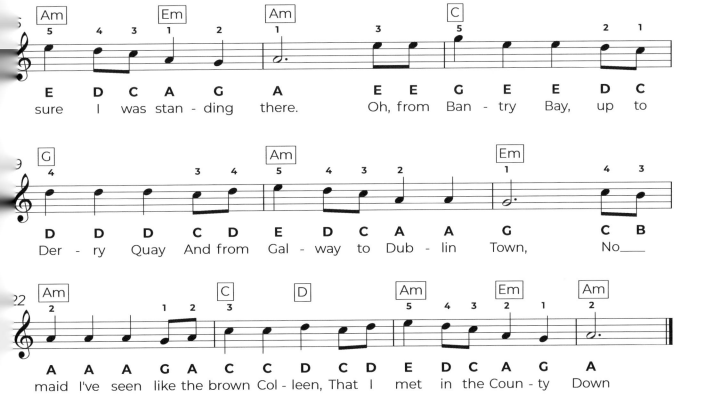

2 As she onward sped I shook my head,
And I gazed with a feeling quare,
And I said, says I, to a passer-by,
"Who's the maid with the nut-brown hair?"
Oh, he smiled at me, and with pride says he,
"That's the gem of Ireland's crown,
She's young Rosie McCann from the banks of
the Bann,
She's the Star of the County Down."

Oh, from Bantry Bay...

3 I've travelled a bit, but never was hit,
Since my roving career began,
But fair and square I surrendered there,
To the charms of young Rose McCann.
I'd a heart to let and no tenant yet,
Did I meet with in shawl or gown,
But in she went and I asked no rent,
From the Star of the County Down.

Oh, from Bantry Bay...

4 At the crossroads fair I'll be surely there,
And I'll dress in my Sunday clothes,
And I'll try sheep's eyes, and deludhering lies,
On the heart of the nut-brown Rose.
No pipe I'll smoke, no horse I'll yoke,
Though with rust my plow turns brown,
Till a smiling bride by my own fireside,
Sits the Star of the County Down.

Oh, from Bantry Bay...

GREENSLEEVES

Traditional

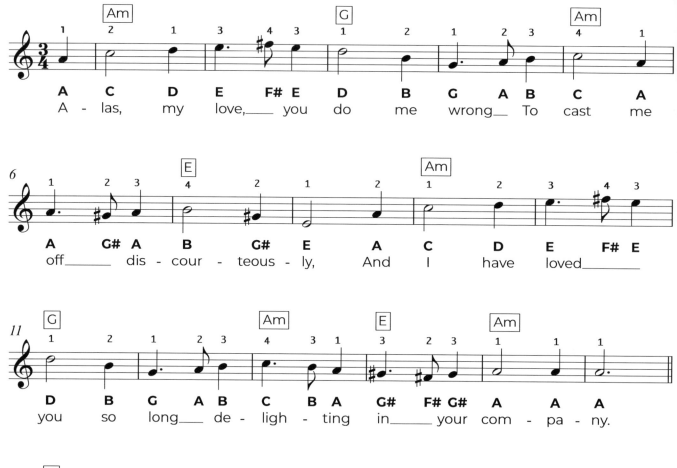

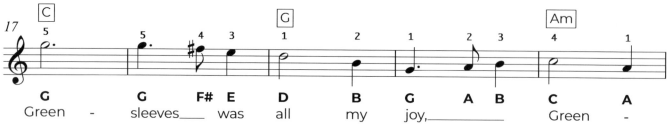

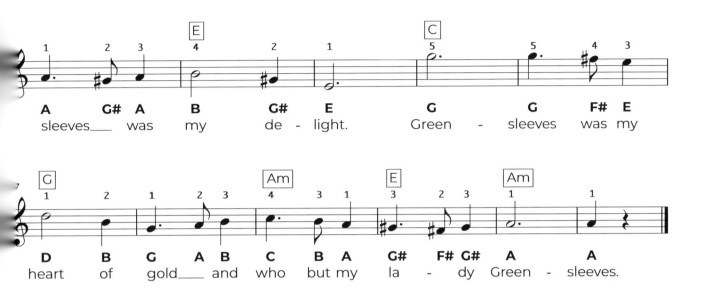

2 I have been ready at your hand,
To grant whatever thou would'st crave,
I have waged both life and land,
Your love and goodwill for to have.

Greensleeves was all my joy...

3 Thy petticoat of slender white
With gold embroidered gorgeously;
Thy petticoat of silk and white
And these I bought gladly.

Greensleeves was all my joy...

4 Thy crimson stockings all of silk,
Wiith gold all wrought above the knee,
Thy pumps as white as was the milk,
And yet thou wouldst not love me.

Greensleeves was all my joy...

5 Greensleeves now farewell adieu,
God I pray to prosper thee,
For I am still thy lover true,
Come once again and love me.

Greensleeves was all my joy...

Take Me Out to the Ball Game

Music: Albert Von Tilze
Lyrics: Jack Norworth

2 Katie Casey saw all the games,
Knew the players by their first names,
Told the umpire he was wrong,
All along,
Good and strong.
When the score was just two to two,
Katie Casey knew what to do,
Just to cheer up the boys she knew,
She made the gang sing this song:

Take me out to the ball game,
Take me out with the crowd,
Buy me some peanuts and Cracker Jack,
I don't care if I never get back,
Let me root, root, root for the home team,
If they don't win, it's a shame,
For it's one, two, three strikes, you're out,
At the old ball game.

Star Spangled Banner

Lyrics: Francis Scott Key
Music: John Stafford Smith

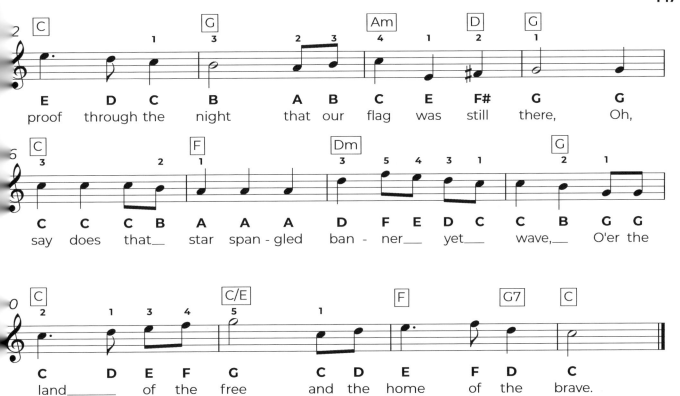

2 On the shore dimly seen through the mists of the deep,
Where the foe's haughty host in dread silence reposes,
What is that which the breeze, o'er the towering steep,
As it fitfully blows, half conceals, half discloses?
Now it catches the gleam of the morning's first beam,
In full glory reflected now shines in the stream,
'Tis the star-spangled banner, O long may it wave,
O'er the land of the free and the home of the brave.

3 And where is that band who so vauntingly swore,
That the havoc of war and the battle's confusion,
A home and a country, should leave us no more?
Their blood has washed out their foul footsteps' pollution.
No refuge could save the hireling and slave,
From the terror of flight, or the gloom of the grave,
And the star-spangled banner in triumph doth wave,
O'er the land of the free and the home of the brave.

4 O thus be it ever, when freemen shall stand,
Between their loved homes and the war's desolation,
Blest with vict'ry and peace, may the Heav'n rescued land,
Praise the Power that hath made and preserved us a nation!
Then conquer we must, when our cause it is just,
And this be our motto: 'In God is our trust,'
And the star-spangled banner in triumph shall wave,
O'er the land of the free and the home of the brave.

It's a Long Way to Tipperary

Jack Judge
Harry Williams

2 Paddy wrote a letter,
To his Irish Molly-O,
Saying, "Should you not receive it,
Write and let me know!
If I make mistakes in spelling,
Molly, dear," said he,
Remember, it's the pen that's bad,
Don't lay the blame on me!"

It's a long way to Tipperary...

3 Molly wrote a neat reply,
To Irish Paddy-O,
Saying "Mike Maloney,
Wants to marry me, and so,
Leave the Strand and Piccadilly,
Or you'll be to blame,
For love has fairly drove me silly,
Hoping you're the same!"

It's a long way to Tipperary...

LOOK FOR THE SILVER LINING

Lyrics: B G De Sylva
Music Jerome Kern

When Irish Eyes are Smiling

Ernest Ba

2 For your smile is a part,
Of the love in your heart,
And it makes even sunshine more bright,
Like the linnet's sweet song,
Crooning all the day long,
Comes your laughter and light.
For the springtime of life,

Is the sweetest of all,
There is ne'er a real care or regret,
And while springtime is ours,
Throughout all of youth's hours,
Let us smile each chance we get.

When Irish eyes are smiling...

Jeanie with the Light Brown Hair

Stephen Foster

I dream of Jea-nie with the light brown hair, Borne like a

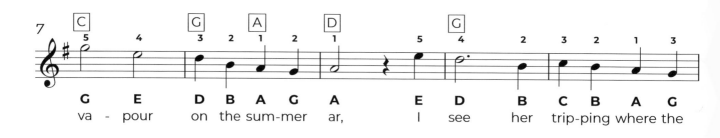

va - pour on the sum-mer ar, I see her trip-ping where the

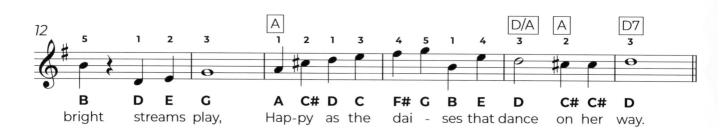

bright streams play, Hap-py as the dai - ses that dance on her way.

Ma - ny were the wild notes her mer - ry voice would pour, Ma-ny were the

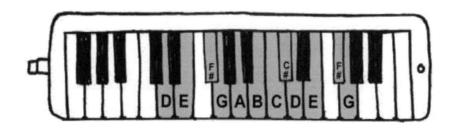

blythe birds that war - bled them o'er, I dream of Jea - nie with the

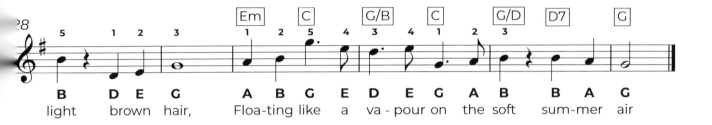

light brown hair, Floa-ting like a va - pour on the soft sum-mer air

2 I long for Jeanie with a day-dawn smile,
Radiant in gladness, warm with winning guile,
I hear her melodies, like joys gone by,
Sighing round my heart over the fond hopes that
die,
Sighing like the night wind and sobbing like the
rain,
Wailing for the lost one that comes not again,
Oh, I long for Jeanie, and my heart bows low,
Never more to find her where the bright waters
flow.

3 I sigh for Jeanie, but her light form strayed,
Far from the fond hearts round her native glade,
Her smiles have vanished and her sweet songs
flown,
Flitting like the dreams that have cheered us and
gone,
Now the nodding wild flowers may wither on the
shore,
While her gentle fingers will cull them no more,
Oh, I sigh for Jeanie with the light brown hair,
Floating, like a vapour, on the soft summer air.

MUSIC THEORY

The essentials of music theory for playing and reading music on the melodica

Note Durations

Music is made up of a series of notes of different lengths, which we call a **RHYTHM**. We measure the duration of a note by counting.

> ## Quarter Note
> (Called *crotchet* in the UK)
> One count long
> Count 'one'

Clap the rhythm below, counting aloud 'one' for each note.

Count: 1   1   1   1

Music is divided into a series of **MEASURSES** or **BARS**, and divided with **BAR LINES**. Clap this rhythm, counting from 1 to 4.

bar line   bar line   bar line

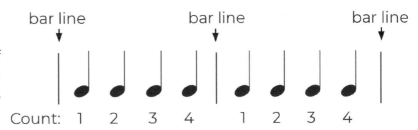

Count: 1   2   3   4   1   2   3   4

This should sound like 8 even claps

> ## Half Note
> (Called *minim* in the UK)
> Two counts long
> Count 'one, two'

Clap this rhythm, counting aloud. Clap once for each note.

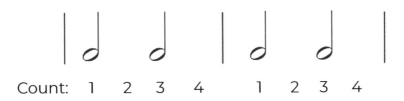

Count: 1   2   3   4   1   2   3   4

This should sound like 4 slow claps

EIGHTH NOTES

Eighth notes have tails, which can join together if there's more than one.

> An eighth note (*quaver* in the UK), is twice as fast as a quarter note *(crotchet* in the UK). 2 eighth notes are played in the time of 1 quarter note.

Clap this rhythm, counting aloud, saying 'and' wherever you see the plus sign.

Count: 1 2 3 4 +   1 2 3 4   1 2 + 3 + 4   1 + 2 3 4

DOTTED QUARTER NOTE
(Called *dotted crotchet* in the UK)
One and a half counts long
Count 'one, and'

A dot after a note adds 50% to the length

Clap this rhythm , counting aloud. Say 'and' where you see a plus sign.

Count: 1 2 + 3 4 +   1 2 + 3 4   1 2 + 3 4 +   1 + 2 3 4

WHOLE NOTE
(Called *semibreve* in the UK)
Four counts long
Count 'one, two, three, four'

Clap this rhythm, counting aloud. Clap once for each note.

Count: 1 2 3 4   1 2 3 4   1 2 3 4   1 2 3 4

This should sound like 4 very slow claps

THE STAFF

Music is written on a group of 5 lines
called a **STAFF**, (or *STAVE* in the UK)

Some notes are written in the spaces between the lines

And some notes are written on the lines

THE TREBLE CLEF

The **TREBLE CLEF** is a sign which shows us where the G line is.
It's sometimes called a G clef, becasue it starts on the G line

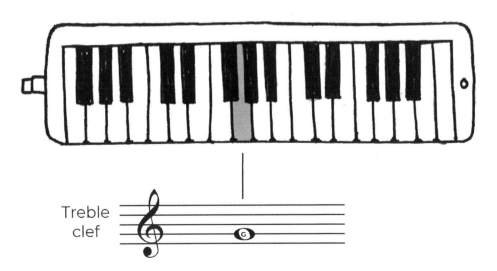

Treble
clef

NOTES ON THE STAFF

Move up and down from the 'G' note to name the other notes

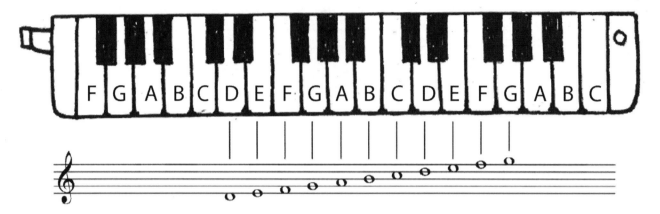

To write the notes that are too
low or too high to fit on the
staff, we add some extra lines

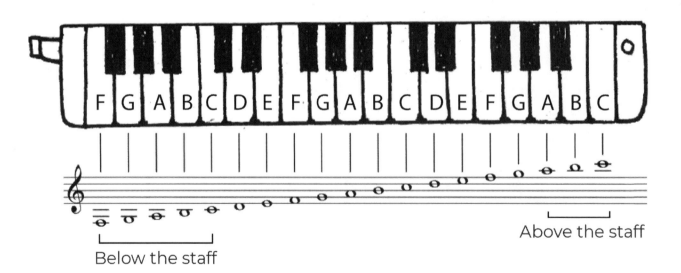

Below the staff

Above the staff

RESTS

QUARTER NOTE REST

est is a sign which
ndicates silence

 This is a quarter rest (*crotchet rest* in the UK)

It indicates silence for the length of a quarter note (*crotchet*)

Clap the following rhythm while counting aloud.
Clap once for each note, and stay silent on the rests.

HALF NOTE REST

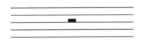 This is a half rest (*minim rest* in the UK)
It lasts for the duration of a half note (*minim*)

WHOLE NOTE REST

This is a whole rest (*semibreve rest* in the UK)
It lasts for the duration of a whole note (*semibreve*),
or a full measure.

SHARPS & FLATS

 The sharp sign before a note means to play the next key to the right. This is normally a black note, but can also be a white note.

A **SHARP** before a note applies every time it re-appears in that measure. It doesn't apply to subsequent measures.

 The flat sign before a note means to play the next key to the left. This is normally a black note, but can also be a white note.

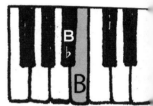

A **FLAT** before a note applies every time it re-appears in that measure. It doesn't apply to subsequent measures.

TIME SIGNATURE

Music has 2 numbers at the beginning, called the **TIME SIGNATURE**

4 means 4 beats in a measure
4 means each beat is a quarter note (*crotchet* in the UK)

3 means 3 beats in a measure
4 means each beat is a quarter note (*crotchet* in the UK)

2 means 2 beats in a measure
4 means each beat is a quarter note (*crotchet* in the UK)

TIED NOTES

When 2 (or more) notes on the same line or space are joined with a curved line, called a **TIE**, the note value becomes the total length of both notes.

This is one note, which lasts for 6 beats (3+3)

PAUSE

 This sign is called a FERMATA or PAUSE. When you see this above a note, you stay on it for a little while

IRREGULAR BARS

Sometimes the first measure of a piece contains less beats than it should. When this happens, the missing beats are made up in the last measure.

SEMITONES AND TONES

A **semitone** or half step is the distance between one key and the next

A **tone** is the distance of 2 semitones

MELODICA RESOURCES

MelodicaWorld.com

Melodicaworld.com is the author's website where you can watch videos and read articles on choosing an instrument, tuning and maintenance, and playing tips.

Melodica World Facebook
melodicaworld.com/fb

Join thousands of players around the world at the Melodica World Facebook group. This is the friendly place to go if you have any questions about your instrument or your playing, or want to show off what you're playing from this book!

Melodica World YouTube
melodicaworld.com/you

I've put together a series of free YouTube Lessons for complete beginners. This is a great place to start learning from scratch.

Melodica Lessons Book One
melodicaworld.com/book

This is the comprehensive melodica tutor for complete beginners. Simple step by step instructions, with online streaming audio - hear how the music in the book should sound, and play along to backing tracks at different speeds.

- A complete musical foundation - music theory and reading
- Play along with the backing tracks - at different speeds
- Suitable for Absolute Beginners - and all ages
- There's musical examples online - hear how the music should sound

This is more than just a 'how-to' book - it's full of inspiring infographics covering::

- Relaxation in performance
- History of the melodica
- Early melodica pioneers
- Melodica in film music
- The art of listening
- How to practice

We cover the names of the notes, note durations, music notation, sharps and flats, key signatures, reggae, waltzes, reading music and everything you need to know to become a great musician.

Made in the USA
Las Vegas, NV
27 December 2023

83576866R00092